Promoting Excellence

Promoting Excellence:

Personnel Management and Staff Development in Libraries

Mary Casteleyn and Sylvia P. Webb

BOWKER
SAUR

London • Melbourne • Munich • New Jersey

British Library Cataloguing in Publication Data

Casteleyn, Mary
      Promoting Excellence: Personnel Management
      and Staff Development in Libraries
      I. Title   II. Webb, Sylvia P.
      023

      ISBN 0-86291-606-2

Library of Congress Cataloging-in-Publication Data

Casteleyn, Mary.
 Promoting excellence: personnel management and staff development
in libraries / Mary Casteleyn and Sylvia P. Webb.
      p.   cm.
 Includes bibliographical references and index.
 ISBN 0-86291-606-2
 1. Libraries--Great Britain--Personnel management.   2. Library
employees--Training of--Great Britain. I. Webb, Sylvia P. II. Title.
Z682.2.G7C37 1993
023.9--dc20   92-38032
                                              CIP

Published by Bowker-Saur, Maypole House, Maypole Road,
East Grinstead, West Sussex RH19 1HH
Tel: +44(0)342 330100 Fax: +44(0)342 330191
Bowker-Saur is a division of REED REFERENCE PUBLISHING

Reprinted 1994

ISBN 0-86291-606-2

Cover design by Pamela Wilson
Typesetting by Joshua Associates Ltd, Oxford
Printed on acid-free paper
Printed and bound in Great Britain by Antony Rowe Ltd, Wiltshire

About the authors

Mary Casteleyn was the Personnel Officer for the Leisure Department of Westminster City Council, UK from 1985–1989 having previously worked as the Personnel Officer for the library service in the same local authority since 1976. Whilst at Westminster she was seconded to work on behalf of the British Council in both India and Malawi developing library training programmes and staff assessment programmes. Since leaving Westminster she has worked as a freelance library personnel and training consultant and been involved in work for many different employers on a contractual basis. She was elected as a national councillor to the Council of the Library Association in 1988 and remains on the Council, serving on the Employment Committee of that organization. She has sat on the Library Association Sub-committee on Training and was co-opted, in 1983, on to the Personnel, Training and Education Group of the Library Association, to assist with the launch of *Training and education: a journal for library and information workers*. Her other publications include *Planning library training programmes* and *Pre-licentiate training guidelines*.

Sylvia P. Webb, now an independent consultant, has worked in a variety of information environments in both the private and the public sectors. She is actively involved in professional education both as Chair of the UK Library Association's Accreditation Board and through her research into current educational activities across a range of other professions. At Ashridge Management College she also lectured in the behavioural sciences, particularly in management and interpersonal skills. She is well-known as both lecturer and writer, two of her best-known titles, *Creating an information service* and *Personal development in information work* having sold in over forty countries. She is a member of several government advisory bodies, and a former Vice-President of the Institute of Information Scientists.

Introduction

Library and information services have always been people-oriented functions, with the user as the central focus. However, without appropriate staff management and development, the service will not meet the user's full requirement, nor will the user become aware of the wide range of services at his or her disposal.

Managing the human resources aspect of an organization's assets is crucial to its success, whatever its objectives and regardless of its setting – i.e. in the private or the public sector. The purpose of this book is to introduce LIS managers to the increasingly complex issues surrounding personnel management in the light of current legislation and practice, and to consider ways of successfully recruiting and retaining staff. The latter is helped considerably by the introduction and implementation of appropriate staff development programmes, particularly where these are part of an overall organizational strategy.

The book is divided into two parts: Part One concentrates on personnel issues such as recruitment and selection, equality of opportunity, performance and appraisal, staff welfare and termination of employment, and underlines the importance of effective communications in employee relations. This is also emphasized in Part Two, which looks at the management of staff training and development, how to assess and plan training and development activities, designing the training programme, quality assurance and performance measurement, as well as considering the manager's own training and development needs.

Throughout the book examples of successful management techniques are given and reference is made to relevant legislation and organizations which can supply further advice and assistance. A number of detailed case studies have been included, showing how local, national and international organizations have developed their own human resources programmes, or managed the introduction of new activities and motivated the staff involved. Reference is also made to other examples which have been described in the professional and management literature. The benefits to both the LIS unit and its parent organization are well illustrated in all these examples, and they will be especially helpful in suggesting ways of managing LIS developments and ensuring that motivated staff with appropriate attitudes and skills are there to take the service forward.

This book will be as useful to experienced LIS specialists who are broadening their organizational role, as to those seeking to acquire or update their skills in the area of human resource management.

Mary Casteleyn and Sylvia P. Webb

Acknowledgements

We would like to thank all those individuals and organizations who responded so willingly to our call for examples of personnel and training documentation. Although it has not been possible to include all of these, we are nevertheless extremely grateful for the interest shown.

Particular thanks are extended to the following for their personal efforts in identifying sources and supplying materials for inclusion: Christine Abbott (Aston University LIS); Andrew Miller (Glasgow City Libraries); Tom Attwood (Cargill Attwood & Thomas Ltd); Derrick Fernandes and Chris Tighe (Westminster Reference Library); Jan Durkin (Melbourne); Philip Kent (CSIRO Melbourne); Gary Knobel (CSIRO Canberra); Jane Hiscock (Southern Australia College of Advanced Education Library, Adelaide); Margaret Trask (Australian Information Management Association, Sydney); Dorothy Cruickshank and Diane Saunders (British Council, Manchester); Lynne Brindley (London School of Economics); Stuart Brewer (Newcastle upon Tyne Leisure Services); Joan Caruso and Constance B. Cooke (Queens Borough Public Library, New York); Peter Cox (City of Westminster Libraries); John Houtman (Dienst Openbare Bibliotheek, Den Haag);

Alison Hunt and Oliver Merrington (Schering Agrochemicals Ltd,); Helene Dang and Gerry Price (Westminster City Council).

Thanks are also due to the Accountancy Library and Information Group; Hertfordshire County Council's Schools Library Service; Westminster Reference Libraries; the Library Association; the American Library Association; Nederlands Bibliotheek en Lektuur Centrum; NFER/Nelson (Routledge); Stoy Hayward; Aslib's Information Resource Centre; ACAS – the Advisory, Conciliation and Arbitration Service; The Industrial Society; The Institute of Personnel Management; The Equal Opportunities Commission.

Without their help, the book would have had far less substance.

Contents

cont'd

Figures

Case studies

PART ONE

Personnel management in library and information services

Mary Casteleyn

CHAPTER ONE

The personnel function: a practical approach

In line with many other organizations, libraries are beginning to introduce policies that refer to citizens' rights and expectations of quality. The delivery of such quality services requires well motivated, well trained and justly rewarded library and information staff, and these three requirements have traditionally been seen as the domain of the human resource manager.

Whereas in large organizations there have been moves towards the devolution of human resource responsibilities to the direct line manager, and an apparent decline in the influence of the centrally controlled personnel function, it is evident that this personnel function now has a far wider and more complex range of responsibilities than ever before. This is reflected in legislative developments at European Community and national levels that affect the way personnel matters can be carried out.

In many local authorities in the UK this is resulting in the corporate human resources function assuming the role of an internal consultancy, selling its specialist services either to the line manager or to the personnel staff who operate at the departmental level. Central human resource staff now operate as facilitators at an executive level, providing a framework for personnel policies, rather than in the traditional role of reacting to demands and performing a variety of routine functions. With the devolution of these routine functions, the centralized human resource unit in large organizations now offers guidance, support and advice to line managers, on a variety of personnel issues. The personnel and training sections of large organizations are having to establish their own ways of monitoring quality control in the services they provide to their 'clients'.

This book aims to provide a broad overview of the personnel function and staff training and development. It is aimed at LIS managers who have little experience of human resource management and who are assuming aspects of the personnel function for the first time, or broadening their management role in this area. It will be just as useful to the manager of a small and isolated information unit as to a librarian operating within a large organization having access to personnel advisers operating at a strategic level. For library managers who have the choice of whether to use an internal or an external supplier of human resource services, it will provide essential background information to aid that decision process.

Compulsory competitive tendering

In the UK recent Local Government Acts [1] contained plans to put out to competitive tender local authority corporate services such as human resource management. Even if this legislation is eventually put into practice for human resource management, the range of personnel work that could be successfully contracted out is still a matter for debate, and could be limited to activities such as recruitment, recruitment advertising and training. Those aspects of human resource management which are part of a manager's normal responsibilities and which require the development of a relationship between the manager and the employee – staff welfare issues, industrial relations and essential in-house training and development, including operational coaching and counselling, for example – are more difficult to isolate from day-to-day management decisions and could be less successfully put out to tender. However, the fact remains that these Local Government Acts reflect a national change of climate in the management and operation of personnel matters, particularly in local government, and line managers need to develop the necessary operational skills and expertise to effectively manage and develop their human resources.

The personnel function

The function of personnel work in any organization will cover:

- Ensuring adequate, competent and suitable personnel
- Defining guidelines for recruitment, appraisal, promotion, termination, equal opportunities, disciplinary procedures, etc.
- Designing a training and development programme
- Ensuring effective employee relations and communications
- Ensuring proper conditions of service and procedures
- Establishing and maintaining proper documentary sources
- Ensuring effective health and safety practices, including staff welfare and working conditions.

Arising from these functions there are three main aspects of human resource work that must always be taken into consideration:

1. The relevant legislation
2. Statutory requirements and constraints affecting employment
3. Operating best professional practice

Reference will be made to these three aspects of human resource management throughout this book. It is essential to be aware of legislation affecting employment and to establish procedures and guidelines that conform to national legislation. It is also important to develop good employee relations, to understand the rights of employees and how these rights should affect managerial decisions. To ensure equity of treatment and consistent management of staff, you will need to establish your own set of guidelines and policies in connection with all aspects of personnel work.

A manual for personnel policies

Whatever the size of your library it is useful to devise a manual which contains the official personnel policies and procedures of the organization. This will help to promote a consistency of approach and can be used as the first point of call when dealing with staffing issues. It will need to be kept up to date and the inserted instructions produced in a standard format, in either colour-coded sections and/or numbered subsections that can easily be removed and revised without affecting the rest of the manual; a ring binder is ideal. The sort of information that you could expect to find in such a manual would be:

- Policies affecting terms and conditions of work, such as hours, overtime rates and special payments
- Employment practices such as advertising, recruitment, selection and appointment procedures
- The creation of and access to the staff files
- Procedures affecting probation, promotions, regrading, appraisals, grievances and disciplinary action
- Salary queries – how it is paid and deductions made
- Pension scheme information
- Staff benefits such as medical insurance, car loans, moving expenses, house-purchase expenses and payments of training fees and expenses
- Holiday and leave entitlements, including leave without pay, sabbatical leave, study leave, leave of absence, sick leave, maternity/paternity leave, jury service leave, etc.

The manual could also usefully include details of the organization, a staff chart and a list of staff telephone extensions, job titles and a brief explanation of individual responsibilities.

Personnel administration

A comprehensive record system is the essential foundation of any personnel service. These records can be maintained manually or on a computer, or on a system which combines the two methods. We will be discussing these records in further detail throughout the book. Records that may be needed will include:

- Comprehensive personnel record files
- Job records, job description files and job evaluations
- Training records and identification of training needs
- Staff appraisal records
- Recruitment and selection documentation
- Records of posts advertised
- Documentation for starters and leavers/retirements
- Records of vacancy levels and staff turnover
- Records of basic pay, overtime, bonus and enhanced pay and salary expenditure

- Records of regrading claims and decisions
- Records of any grievance or disciplinary cases

Staff at work also have certain statutory rights and you will need to develop clear policies and procedures to cover these and to maintain records in these areas:

- Equal opportunities
- Sickness/absence policies, including statutory sick pay
- Pre-natal and maternity leave and pay policies
- Disciplinary and grievance procedures
- Holiday and special leave entitlements
- Health, safety, medical and welfare policies
- Staff training and development policies
- Termination and redundancy procedures

You are required by statute to maintain some staffing records including, for example, records of salaries and wages, tax deductions and payments for sickness or maternity reasons, although these may be held by a central personnel department. Some employee statutory rights do not necessarily need continuity or length of service on behalf of the member of staff; these include a written statement of details of employment, medical suspension pay and the right to a written statement of pay details. Employee rights under the Race Relations Act 1976 and the Sex Discrimination Act 1972 are discussed in Chapter 2.

Drafting and issuing employment letters, including offers of employment, letters of termination, disciplinary and welfare letters, is an important part of personnel work. If you are unused to compiling these and need guidance and advice, then publications such as *Ready drafted employment letters* by Barraclough and Nilsson [2] or those produced by the Advisory, Arbitration and Conciliation Service, such as *Employing people; the ACAS handbook for small firms* [3] or *Discipline at work: the ACAS advisory handbook* [4] contain useful draft letters, statements and contracts.

Personnel files

Personnel files are usually opened after an offer of a job has been accepted. Even when a computerized personnel system is in operation, it is still effective to maintain manual staff files containing the application forms, copies of qualifications, signed acceptances of the post and the written job offers, which constitute legal documents. Although some computer companies will tell you that you do not need to maintain manual files, and encourage you to microfilm those you already have, this may not be cost-effective or prudent. You also need to take note of the requirements of the Data Protection Act in the UK, and the privacy legislation of other countries regarding computerized personal data if operating outside the UK. At European Community level a draft directive to harmonize member states' data protection legislation signals a Europe-wide awareness of the importance of privacy.

One of the benefits of computerized personnel systems is in the rapid and detailed analysis of staffing statistics used for human resource planning, for example age profiling or staff turnover rates. Another benefit is that data on a member of staff need only be listed once but can be used for a variety of purposes, such as monitoring sickness absences and, if connected to the payroll system, to feed in information about those absences that affect salary and wage payments. Manually maintaining and updating such records and completing returns is a necessary but time-consuming and lengthy process; if such records are to be kept on a computerized personnel system for possible transmission on to another department, such as the finance department, you will need to ensure that any system you choose will be compatible with the organizational system. If planning a computerized system you must produce a precise user specification of your requirements and undertake proper market research before finalizing any purchase; you will also need to undertake a proper cost justification statement. However, whatever system you decide to use, the content of the files will need to be the same.

Usually a detailed file for each member of staff is kept by the personnel department. In some libraries, a more compact file listing personal details is kept by the library manager. Wherever these files are located they must be securely kept, ideally in a locked filing cabinet; confidentiality of computerized personnel files must be strictly maintained, with access via a confidential password restricted to authorized staff. It is vital that the information contained in these files is up to date, relevant to the employment history and to the employer/employee relationship. If maintaining a manual file, you may find it useful to summarize such information on a separate sheet, which can readily be extracted from the file.

The content of the personnel file should include:

- Personal information about the employee: current work and home address, telephone numbers, next of kin to be contacted in an emergency. This last entry will need to be regularly checked to ensure it is up to date. Should you ever need to contact a next of kin it will invariably be during normal working hours, so you will need to have a daytime address and telephone number.
- Application form for the post, letter of appointment (which includes all the details of the post), the employee's letter of acceptance and the conditions of work. If not included in the letter of appointment, you should also include details of the start date, salary, date of first pay increment and other financial agreements. Any references received and the medical clearance should also be included in the file.
- A copy of the job description, signed and dated by the employee.
- Documents that relate to changes of status of the employee, such as promotions or transfers, salary changes, changes of job title and records of requests for changes which have come from the employee.
- Documents that relate to performance, such as appraisal evaluations, which include statements from both the employee and the manager. Documents that refer to any disciplinary action will also be kept in the personnel file, although retention of these will be limited by a time factor.
- A section should also be maintained for particular information about training and development programmes and any training and education completed, especially if this will affect salary payments. Such information is also useful if you need to write a reference on behalf of the employee. Copies of references supplied to other employers should also be maintained in the file.
- Records must be maintained relating to absences from work; although the day-to-day record may not be kept on the file you will eventually need to record any extended leave of absence, say for jury service, educational leave and extended sick leave.
- Finally, documents relating to termination of employment must be kept on the file, including the letter of resignation or retirement and a copy of your letter of acknowledgement. Most importantly, a forwarding address should be noted.

Ledvinka and Scarpello in *Federal regulations of human resource management* [5] suggest subdividing personnel files into separate sections in order to protect the privacy of the information in each section. The creation of separate sections on performance and appraisal information, disciplinary information, payroll/salary information and medical information, would prevent anyone using the file for legitimate purposes, such as a payroll clerk, having immediate access to confidential information that had no relevance to the work in hand.

The Data Protection Act 1984 in the UK gives the employee right of access to any information held about them on a computerized system. It is important, in the UK, not to confuse this with an automatic right to access everything held in a manual file. In the USA, the Privacy Act 1974 protects federal government employees' rights to determine, review and correct information which is being held, and to prevent information being used for any purpose other than that for which it was collected; several states have passed laws relating to access to personnel files. This is further discussed by Ledvinka and Scarpello [5], as is the implication of potential conflicts of interest arising from the US Freedom of Information Act. Although this Act does contain an exception for personnel files, in practice the courts have on occasion overruled the public's right to privacy in favour of the public's right to know. The American Library Association [6] has issued guidelines which cover a range of issues about the recording and storing of personnel information. In these the personnel file is defined as the official record of the employee's work history and training; this definition is important, since the records kept in personnel files must only relate to the employee's employment history and it is good practice to ensure that this is the case. However, in order to create realistic and enforceable expectations about the confidentiality of the personnel files and disclosures from them, you should consider the creation of a written policy relating to the contents of the files and access to them by other staff, or by the employee themself; for example, the Glasgow City Libraries Employee Assessment and Development Scheme case study in Part Two makes specific reference to the retention of employee assessment and development forms, and the restrictions on their use. A policy statement on personnel files should include:

- Lists of types of material maintained in the files and the reasons for its retention or withdrawal.
- Lists of documents available to the employee: this would exclude references written in confidence. Also information that may be

released from the file without the employee's permission, and what information would require such permission.

- A procedure if the employee wishes to see their own file. An employee may wish to have such access to check details of their work history before making an application for another post, or to check that the file is up to date. In some organizations the employee has to give at least 24 hours' notice and the file may be inspected only in the presence of the personnel officer, to prevent the unauthorized addition or extraction of material.
- A list of post-holders to whom the files can be released and a procedure if a staff file is needed by a senior member of staff – to write a reference, or to check the last appraisal assessment. A system of booking files in and out must be established to ensure that none go astray.
- A system for updating information held in the file, such as promotions, transfers, salary increases. In a computerized system this can be relatively easy, but may be more cumbersome in a manual system. Updating also means withdrawing material no longer needed on the file, such as spent disciplinary actions.
- A decision on how long to maintain a file after the employee has left. There is no specific statutory requirement about the retention of personnel files, but details of salary and wages payments will be kept as part of the normal accounting records, as will details of any pension contributions or payments. In the UK, under the Disabled Persons (Employment) Act 1944, as amended in 1958, employers who are subject to the quota system, or who have designated employment for disabled people, are required to keep staff records (though not necessarily the staff files) for 2 years from the period to which they relate. This requirement is discussed in detail in Chapter 2.

Some files are held indefinitely in an archive section; others are destroyed after a reasonable period of time – say 6 years – although if this happens details should be kept of the names of former staff and their periods of employment; according to circumstances, files may be needed to write references for former members of staff, or later to draft obituaries. Before destroying any file, it is good practice to consider whether the time limits for claims that could be made against you as an employer have expired, otherwise you will be destroying information that you may need to access at some later stage. The American Library Association guidelines [6] recommend that, since the file provides a historical record of the employee's relationship it should be normally retained indefinitely – particularly files containing information of permanent importance about former employees.

The destroying of the files of former employees, or the discarding of confidential staff information, such as disciplinary records, must be handled effectively so that information cannot fall into the wrong hands – shredding ensures that this will not happen.

In some large organizations general record files are maintained that relate to specific types of staffing issues – thus sickness records, which have an immediate financial implication, may need to be kept separately from the personnel file, as are records of annual holidays. Accident reports and medical records may also be kept separately, since these have been completed in confidence and require professional medical interpretation. Other staffing records relating to race, sex or disability which can be used to help eliminate discrimination may also be needed to be kept separately, usually in statistical form rather than under the name of the employee.

Human resource planning

Whatever sort of library you manage, one of the most important responsibilities you have will relate to the staff you employ. Having responsibility for staff means having responsibility for one of the most expensive assets of the organization. The first step in using the staffing assets effectively is to relate personnel planning to the current and future needs of the organization or library, and to do this within the context of the corporate plan as well as the LIS business plan.

The overall corporate plan or your individual library plan will allow you to assess your staffing requirements for known objectives within a set timescale. This assessment of need can then be evaluated against a current audit of staff. To carry out a staff audit you will need information relating to age, experience, skills, talents and aptitude, much of which is probably already available, either in the personnel files or will have been gleaned from regular staff assessments and appraisals. This audit will allow you to compare what human resources are available – including the surfeit or deficiency of skills – with the skills that will be needed to effectively operate the forward plan for the library. You will need to bear in mind that it is as wasteful and non-productive to employ over-qualified staff as it is to employ under-qualified personnel.

The divergence of skills shown up by the audit will indicate the need for either recruiting new staff or retraining existing staff.

Effective human resource planning should lead to improved balancing of recruitment needs and the avoidance of long delays in getting projects off the ground due to not having suitable staff available at the right time. Additionally, this means evaluating what needs to be done for existing staff in order for them to fulfil the requirements of any forward planning. Options to consider and which may need to have policies developed include:

- Training and retraining
- Redeployment
- Job enhancement, promotion and/or succession planning
- Organizational and structural staffing changes
- Offers of early retirement.

Staff training and development is an integral part of human resource planning, representing as it does a further investment in the human resources of the organization. Any definition of the skills needed to operate the LIS forward plan and the review of the staff audit will have identified a need for a wide variety of training, as will the normal recruitment processes and regular staff appraisals. Human resource planning should lead to planned and purposeful training and development of the existing library staff, as is discussed later in this book.

Another essential source of information for human resource planning are the statistical records that should be maintained in relation to personnel work, which will give you an indication of what may or may not be possible. These will include useful statistics on:

- Staff turnover rates
- Vacancy levels
- Absence and sickness levels
- Effective recruitment sources and advertising media
- Problems encountered in recruiting certain types of staff
- Market conditions, rates of pay and conditions of work.

Human resource planning, should not be viewed as a one-off exercise in relation to a specific business or corporate plan. Like those business and corporate plans, which are monitored and under constant review, human resource planning must be regarded as an ongoing and continuing process which needs regular updating, adaptation and evaluation.

The Institute of Personnel Management [7] has issued a statement which provides excellent introductory advice and guidelines for managers seeking to introduce human resource planning into their organizations.

Developing an employment policy

One of the areas that can come under stringent review and intense pressure in times of economic stress is the cost of staffing. Human resource planning becomes even more important because library and information work is so labour-intensive. As well as examining the skills, experience and competencies needed by the staff, human resource planning means taking informed decisions about the number of staff required, the hours of work needed and the translation of the value of that work into salaries and wages.

Staffing and employment costs

Your organization's employment policy will require you to have a clear and strategic overview of the true costs of employing staff. Salary and wages expenditure should be carefully and regularly monitored, usually on a monthly basis – it may not be to your advantage to either over or underspend on the salaries budget: indeed, it would be seen as poor planning in most libraries if you failed to manage within the staffing budget. In any case, a good manager should always know the exact amount of money spent on staffing costs in any one year, per site or per project. This is essential in order to project and justify your future budget. You will need to understand the true human resource costs in order to estimate whether it will be cheaper or more cost-effective to employ a temporary worker, or to pay overtime, or to create a new post in order to meet a specific need.

It is very tempting to evaluate the cost of staff by simply assuming that existing salaries and wages, plus allowances for projected pay rises, are the only figures that need to be taken into account. Consideration of the initial salary alone of a new permanent staff member is not enough, but rather the true cost to the organization if that member of staff stays in post and reaches the top of their scale or performance rating. Thus in producing an annual staffing budget based on the fixed costs of posts, it is usual practice to base the overall budget calculations on the penultimate or final points of salary scales. This will give a good realistic average of costs per year. The fixed costs of any staffing budget are those which will only vary with the number of staff employed, and not the hours worked. Allowances may also have to be made for forward planning on pay awards.

You will also need to examine costs other than the fixed costs, such as overtime, shift payments, bonus and merit payments. Overtime, if paid at one and a half times the normal rate or at double time, unless allowed for, can quickly overstretch any budget. For this reason overtime payments should be carefully monitored and, if they are proving excessively expensive, you should consider whether the work requiring the overtime could be completed by a different method – for example hiring extra temporary staff or by asking existing staff to work extra shifts in return for time off in lieu.

Payroll administrative costs

Linked to the actual salaries and wages are the administrative costs, which will include the statutory employer's contribution of national insurance – a non-fixed cost in the UK but comparable to a fixed cost in the USA – and which may also include the employer's pension contribution to the employee's fund. Each organization will be slightly different, but these unavoidable administrative costs may add on as much as 17%–20% of the real cost of each salary and wage. Included here should be the true cost of holidays, earlier entitlements to sick and maternity payments and provision for any voluntary social welfare benefits, provision of meal vouchers, subsidized transport, health care and employer's liability insurance. As Rothwell and Mingard (*Comparative labour costs of employing permanent staff and using temporary workers through agencies*), [8] state, the total costs to an organization of employing permanent staff is frequently grossly underestimated, and it is not unusual for total costs to amount to over 50% more than basic wage or salary costs. Other hidden costs involved will include the administrative time of line managers and/or personnel staff, and the overheads of office accommodation. Training is another important aspect of staffing costs. Not all these 'hidden costs' will actually appear in the salary budget; nevertheless it is vital to be aware of them.

Staff turnover rates

Use of the known turnover rate in calculating the annual staffing budget is a legitimate financial tool; this means calculating that a certain proportion of your posts will not be filled for a period of time during the year, and allowing for this 'saving' in the final staff budget. The staff turnover rate can be critical in calculating the cost of replacements: for example, if the turnover rate is high you can safely assume that a proportion of your staff will never reach the top of their particular salary scale, and therefore, in effect, your staff costs will always be low because the staff are nearly always at the beginning of the pay scale. This, of course, will have its drawbacks since a high staff turnover rate may lead to low or loss of productivity, and a period of high unemployment could seriously upset this calculation, since staff may not leave but remain in post, and thus become more expensive as they work their way up the salary scales. Apart from the financial implications you will need to forecast the turnover rates in order to assess any future staffing needs.

In evaluating staffing costs you should bear in mind recruitment costs and the exit costs of previous employees. Exit costs will involve not only a reduction in efficiency and output for the length of time the post is vacant, but also the induction and training costs for new staff, and the time for exit interviews, termination paperwork and the production of references. Taking all these costs into account, it may sometimes be cheaper and more effective to employ temporary personnel or staff from an agency. Although at first sight employing agency staff may look expensive, it involves the employer in no administrative or hidden costs such as sickness or holiday pay – the employer simply signs a time-sheet once a week and pays the agency's bill, usually a percentage on top of the rate of paid by them to the employee. If you examine the true costs of your permanent staff, over and above the salaries paid, the actual costs of using agency staff for specific projects may in fact be cost-effective.

Job analysis and design

A systematic programme of job design, work restructuring and organizational analysis permits the construction of jobs that are rewarding and satisfying to the staff and effective in the delivery of the service. To optimize the use of staff you must employ the right mix of staff to do the right jobs, and provide working conditions to allow them to operate properly. To define the skill and knowledge needed in the staff you must first fully understand the nature of the work they do; for this you will need to conduct job analysis on a task-by-task survey of the work performed.

This can be done by asking staff to keep, over a period of time, records of all tasks performed and the amount of time spent on those tasks. Some observation by the person undertaking the job analysis and on-the-job interviews will assist in identification of the tasks and their relative importance. You should try to identify which aspects of a job are time-consuming, complex and the most difficult, although this latter point may indicate a training need. Exit interviews can be useful in undertaking ongoing research into job analysis, and although the replies may sometimes be subjective, they may lead you to consider redesigning the post or redistributing the workload. Job design is not solely about efficiency and effectiveness, but also about creating jobs which provide some degree of job satisfaction and a quality working environment for the staff.

Once you have a list of all the tasks you will be able to consider redesigning the jobs by grouping tasks together in a different way. Job restructuring involves breaking the job down into all its component parts and putting it together again to achieve definite and improved objectives; if you are creating a new post, you will be able to identify and describe the tasks or parts of the job that need to be done, within the context of the LIS objectives or business plan.

In terms of work allocation and the number of working hours available, it is prudent to think in terms of employing staff with a degree of flexibility and considering whether in fact full-time or full-time equivalent posts are needed – this will involve the same number of working hours but perhaps not the same number of people. Employing more part-time staff would allow you to use the staff with more flexibility, for example, the splitting of one full-time post into two or more part-time posts might allow you to use time more productively by separating the professional from the clerical work, and then paying two members of staff at two different rates of pay. Employing two or three part-time staff instead of one full-time person enables you to schedule all those staff to be on duty together at the busiest times. This flexible use of staffing allows access to a wider mix of staffing skills and experience.

Finally, having analysed all the tasks and designed or redesigned the jobs, the next task is to draft the job descriptions.

Writing a job description

A *job description* reflects the content of the job exactly *as it is*; *job specifications* reflect the situation as it is *intended or thought* to be. Most job descriptions follow similar formats and to design a job description you must:

- Decide the main function and purpose of the post.
- Decide on and list the aims/objectives/ accountabilities of the post to achieve the job purpose; the number of these will vary. Some posts only have 2–4 main aims/objectives/accountabilities, which may subdivide into a larger number of actual activities/tasks. The example shown below has 11 accountabilities.
- List all job activities/tasks, or the job content needed to achieve those aims/objectives/accountabilities.
- Decide which part of the job content or the activities/tasks are the most important: not all parts of the job will be of the same value or take the same amount of time.
- List the job content/activities/tasks in a logical order which relates to the order of the aims/objectives or accountabilities.

A job description will normally show the location of the post and a reporting structure, that is, the post or person to whom the post-holder reports and the number of staff supervised. A decision is also taken about a job title and a job/post number if the organization has a large staffing structure.

An excellent job description, which covers all the above points and is an example of good practice, is reproduced below with the kind permission of Schering Agrochemicals Limited, Chesterford Park Research Station, Saffron Walden, Essex CB10 1XL. (Schering Agrochemicals Limited is part of Schering AG, Germany.)

Job Description – Schering

Job title
Librarian

Job holder
(Name of post-holder to be inserted)

Function	*Department*
Research and development	Library services
Location	*Reports to*
Chesterford Park	Library Services Supervisor

1. Job Purpose Statement

To ensure that the library services meet the requirements of the Research Station and ensure that they evolve to meet the continuously changing challenges of a research environment.

2. Job Context

The library services at Chesterford Park consist of a central library and information service. The library contains a wide collection of general and reference books, journals and reprints, covering the scientific and commercial interests of the Company, together with additional materials held by research departments. The library is responsible for displaying, circulating, organising a loan service, storing and informing staff of the availability of these materials. The Librarian is responsible for the purchase of all published materials. The library staff provide a service for classifying, cataloguing and indexing of all materials, and for relevant photocopying. The library provides advice and assistance to management and departmental specialists on the latest developments in library procedures and equipment.

3. Organisation

Your immediate superior	–	Library Services Supervisor
You and your peers	–	Job holder
Your subordinates	–	Assistant to the Librarian

4. Job Accountabilities

4.1   To carry out all duties with due regard for the health and safety of all staff and of non company people. This includes adherence to COSHH (Control of Substances Hazardous to Health)

4.2   Provide a prompt service for the purchase and distribution of all new books, journals, reprints and other published materials required by the Company

4.3   Maintain the book and journal collections and ensure they are readily accessible to meet and satisfy users needs

4.4   Maintain standing orders for departments at Chesterford Park, Hauxton and Mount Pleasant

4.5   Maintain Library Catalogue (ASSASSIN) ensuring that materials can be found easily

4.6   Give guidance and specialist advice in matters relating to copyright

4.7   Maintain coordination with the decentralised information units within the Company

4.8   Provide a book/journal information service and information retrieval services by using both online and manual sources

4.9   Ensure that all library users are aware of the library and what it has to offer. Arrange library tours and organise training as appropriate

4.10 Ensure that the central library is operating effectively and making the best use of staff and resources. Make recommendations for improvements as necessary

4.11 Promote new services, e.g. handle enquiries relating to the business and commercial world

5. Decision Making Authority

Without Reference: Acts as buyers of published materials for the Company

Decides which supplier of publications to use

Approves invoices up to £500

| | Decisions relating to the day-to-day running of the library |
| With Reference: | Decides which books and journals to purchase for the library |

6. Job Content

6.1 Be consistently on the lookout for potential hazards and act promptly to remove the hazard personally or report it. Handle reprographic chemicals with due regard for COSHH

6.2 Organise and operate a purchasing system, to ensure that materials requested by staff can be promptly supplied. Co-ordinate purchasing for other departments to ensure that unnecessary multiple acquisition of books etc. is avoided

6.3 Organise and operate a comprehensive classification, cataloguing and indexing system for all published materials in the company. Ensure that all materials are displayed adequately and that books are properly handled and stored

6.4 Renew standing orders for annual publications or materials with updates. Check invoices and pass them to appropriate department heads for approval

6.5 Act as System Administrator for the Library Catalogue (ASSASSIN). Liaise with MIS Department over system amendments, act as troubleshooter. Maintain system so that it runs efficiently. Train staff in its use, as appropriate

6.6 Keep up to date with current legislation on Copyright, attend meetings and liaise with colleagues in the world of information and librarianship to answer any queries etc. raised by members of staff

6.7 Answer enquiries by means of regular meetings and liaison with information staff based in other departments

6.8 Provide personally or through trained staff a means of answering bibliographic queries raised by staff by using hardback sources, catalogues etc. and online databases

6.9 Ensure staff awareness of Library Service by personal contact and good communication skills. Arrange training and library tours/instruction as required

6.10 Keep up to date in the latest library techniques by attending meetings, conferences and through reading journals. Analyse existing procedures and make cost-effective improvements. Supervise staff to maintain an effective service to users

6.11 Build up experience in using online sources. Talk to colleagues who are searching, attend courses in business and information

7. Quantitative Data

(a) financial data   . . . . .
(b) total number of employees for whom you have
     line responsibility   One
(c) other data   . . . . .

8. Job Challenges

To ensure that all potential users of the service are aware of the services provided by the Library and to ensure that a high level of customer satisfaction is generated

9. Relationships (apart from line manager and subordinates)

— Maintain direct contact with all members of staff up to Director level for provision of reference materials, answering queries or advising on library systems
— Maintain contact with staff nominated by Group Leaders who control the purchase of books and journals
— Maintain contacts with external libraries subscription agents, booksellers, publishers and bookbinders

10. Job Knowledge, Skills and Experience

Graduate qualification in science with postgraduate qualification in librarianship studies, or graduate qualification in librarianship studies with at least two years' postgraduate experience in a library, preferably an industrial library, or at least five years practical experience in commercial library work

Ability to read written German would be helpful but not essential

Ability to communicate effectively in writing and verbally with staff at all levels

Ability to motivate and train subordinates, as appropriate

> 11. *Additional Information*
>
> . . . .
>
> *Job Description agreed by*:
> Post Holder   Date
> Line Manager   Date

This very clear job description, set against the context of the job, is particularly useful; the employee will have no doubt about areas of responsibility since decisions which can be made independently without reference are listed, as are the job challenges and the responsibility for communicating with all levels of staff. It is interesting, in the light of continuing professional development, that responsibility for keeping up to date professionally and attending courses and conferences is built into the job description as part of the job content.

Definition of library staff work activities

Clarification about whether the content of a post can be categorized as at professional or paraprofessional/library assistant level can usually be obtained from the professional LIS association. A statement of policy adopted by the Council of the American Library Association [9] recommends categories of library personnel, including library clerks and technical assistants, and the level of training and education appropriate to each of these categories. The nature of suitable job responsibilities is listed against each level. This statement further clarifies the use of job titles to make clear the level of the employee's qualifications, and defines the title of 'librarian' as one carrying with it the connotation of 'professional', in the sense that professional tasks are those that require special background and education in order to identify, analyse, plan, formulate, communicate and administer successful library programmes of service to users. In the UK The Library Association has produced a guide for employers [10] which carries a similar definition of a professional librarian, and gives a description of the required skills and activities as well as a note on professional qualifications. Both the above publications would be helpful in job design and in drafting job descriptions.

Job evaluation

Job evaluation, although not an exact science, is a traditional and long-established method of reaching a fair assessment of the value of a job for grading and pay purposes. The job description is the first document that is needed in the process of evaluating a post for basic salary grading, although a final remuneration may be also affected by market factors or by comparison with similar jobs elsewhere. Other factors that need to be examined, and which are to be found in one way or another in a large variety of job evaluation schemes, are:

- The amount of personal responsibility in the post
- The complexity of the tasks performed and the pace of work
- The training needed to perform the job
- The knowledge, skills and abilities required
- The scope for independent/creative thought
- The span, complexity and level of analytical thought
- The number of staff supervised and supervision received
- Level of contacts within/outside the organization
- Budgetary/financial responsibilities

These processes of analysis scrutinize all the factors of the post so that no part of it is overlooked or the final evaluation based on one or more predominant features. Many evaluation schemes operate by evaluating the separate components of a job and allocating a score to those components. The uniform application of predetermined numerical values ensures the measuring of all tasks by the same yardstick, and helps to guard against intuitive judgements and bias by the evaluators. The addition of the component scores produces an overall total score which serves to grade the post and to allocate a salary. There may also be other factors to take into consideration, such as scarcity of skills or market rates. However, any evaluation scheme will be only as good and as fair as the evaluators allow it to be; even when proper training to implement a job evaluation scheme has taken place, intentional and unintentional bias can creep into the process. This point and the use of subjective judgements are further discussed by Charles Johnson *et al.* in *Equal pay for work of equal value* [11].

There are simpler job evaluation methods, such as job ranking or classification, when each job is considered as a whole rather than analysed, and placed in a ranking order. These methods are effective if dealing with small numbers of staff but not in larger or more complex organizations. ACAS [12] produce a useful booklet which discusses different methods of job evaluation in more detail.

The Equal Pay Act 1970 and the Equal Pay (Amendment) Regulations 1983 in the UK enable a woman to claim the right to treatment equal to that given to male employees if she does work of a similar nature, or a job which has been rated equivalent under a job evaluation scheme. European legislation also affects equal pay rights. The right of equal pay for work of equal value calls for careful examination of any job evaluation procedures, to eliminate any sex bias which could be interpreted as discriminatory.

References

1. *Local Government Acts*. (1988–1992) London: HMSO
2. Barraclough, Mike and Nilsson, John A. (1991) *Ready drafted employment letters*. Cambridge: Director Books
3. Advisory, Conciliation and Arbitration Service (1990). *Employing people: the ACAS handbook for small firms*. London: ACAS
4. Advisory, Conciliation and Arbitration Service (1987). *Discipline at work: the ACAS advisory handbook*. London: ACAS
5. Ledvinka, James and Scarpello, Vida G. (1991) *Federal regulations of human resource management*. Boston: Kent
6. American Library Association *Personnel files guidelines*. ALA Library Administration and Management Association. Chicago.
7. Institute of Personnel Management (1991) *Human resource planning: an IPM statement*. London: IPM
8. Rothwell, Sheila and Mingard, Paul. *Comparative labour costs of employing permanent staff and using temporary workers through agencies*. London: The Federation of Recruitment and Employment Services Ltd.
9. American Library Association (1970) *Library education and personnel utilization: a statement of policy adopted by the council of the American Library Association*. Chicago: ALA
10. Library Association (1991) *Professional librarians: a brief guide for employers*. London: The Library Association
11. Johnson, Charles *et al.* (1991) *Equal pay for work of equal value: a guide to the non-discriminatory use of job evaluation*. British Psychological Society
12. Advisory, Conciliation and Arbitration Service (1991) *Job evaluation: an introduction*. London: ACAS

CHAPTER TWO

Recruitment and selection procedures

In any organization there should be progressive and uniform selection procedures to ensure a high standard of recruitment. This entails determining and then developing and maintaining the procedures which best suit your own library or information service. Poor staff recruitment procedures will affect the efficiency of the library or information service; selecting the wrong staff will increase turnover, leading to low morale and low productivity, both of which affect the quality of the service to the public.

The costs of recruitment

First of all you will need an understanding of the true costs of staff recruitment, selection and replacement. Apart from the obvious expense of advertising, you may also be involved in headhunting costs, selection testing and the use of assessment centres and medical examinations. Candidates' justifiable expenses can include travel to the place of interview, subsistence and perhaps hotel costs, and any hospitality offered by your library. Add to this the cost of staff time involved in the recruitment and interview processes at both managerial and administrative levels, plus the hidden costs of loss of productivity whilst the post is vacant, and adaptation time for the new member of staff, and you will begin to understand the overall cost in real terms to the organization.

Job analysis and job description

As we have seen in the previous chapter, job analysis assists in the preparation of the job description and affects the rate of pay for the post. Reviewing the job description, or compiling one if none exists, is axiomatic to the recruitment process. A successful outcome to selection procedures can only be achieved if you know exactly what the job entails – if you are not clear about the content of the job, you will be unclear about the level of education, the skills and competencies required of the person needed to fill that post. As well as this you will need to analyse the post in organizational terms, that is, where it fits in the overall plan. Successful interviewing and selection procedures depends on these preliminary investigations.

Person specifications

A person specification is a profile of the essential and desirable attributes required of a candidate for the effective performance of duties in a specific post. Although it is unlikely that any candidate will meet all the requirements exactly, the compilation of the person specification helps to clarify what is needed, and this in turn makes the advertising and interview procedures much easier. In the UK, the person specification usually follows a seven-point plan, introduced originally in 1930 by Professor Alec Rodger but not published until 1952 [1]. This approach, quoted with kind permission of NFER-Nelson, specified the desired requirements of a candidate under seven headings: physical make-up, attainments, general intelligence, special aptitudes, interests, disposition and circumstances. Rawling (1985) [2] discusses how this scheme has developed and changed since it was first introduced, and updates the text to take account of new social attitudes and modern occupational psychology. However, the basic seven-point approach retains its value as a useful tool for interviewers to assess the potential of a possible employee. The personal specification would normally include a statement of ideal requirements under the following headings:

- Physical atttributes necessary for the job, such as a clear speaking voice
- Educational attainments and qualifications
- Assessment of intelligence and alertness

- Special aptitudes, such as organizational ability, language skills etc.
- Interests that might be helpful to the job
- Disposition and personality
- Personal circumstances – availability for work or ability to travel or work shifts etc.

To avoid unnecessary discrimination, the content of the person specification must relate directly to the specific needs of the job and to the requirements necessary to operate effectively in that post. The person specification is an internal working document and not made available to the candidates. Indeed, as stated by Bolton *Interviewing for selection decisions* [3], there is a case for *not* giving applicants the full person specification as they might then try to distort the picture of themselves to fit the specification.

Methods of recruitment

A value judgement must be made about where and how to advertise the vacancy to target suitable applicants. In some cases this may mean advertising in the local or national press, or in professional or other specialized journals. Factors to bear in mind are the circulation of the publication, the size and style of the advertisement, the cost and any time delay before the advertisement appears in print. Some local or national newspapers carry job vacancies once a week, and some professional journals may only reach potential applicants on a fort-nightly or monthly basis – this has the effect of lengthening the recruitment process but will be more effective if it reaches people who might be suitable for the post.

If your library has any agreement with existing staff to advertise posts internally, then it is advisable to advertise externally simultaneously. Restrictive practices, such as internal advertisement only, result in poor staff selection since the applicants are never reviewed against the outside market and no new blood is brought into the organization, except at the most preliminary levels. Advertising by word of mouth only can lead to charges of discrimination; advertising by putting up notices in the library or within the wider organization can be helpful if used in addition to other recruitment methods. Restricting applications to internal candidates (or ring fencing as it is sometimes called) is only valid when you are attempt-ing to redeploy staff facing redundancy.

For some posts it may be more effective to place the vacancy in the local Job Centres. This is a service free to the employer and would normally draw on a pool of local people. Commercial employment agencies charge a minimum of 10% of the starting salary for every employee they place, although there is no charge if they fail to fill the vacancy, and they are not necessarily cost-effective for staff that can be easily accessed via other routes. In the UK the specialist employment agencies, such as the Library Association INFOMATCH Recruitment Agency, or organizations such as Task Force Pro Libra Ltd (TFPL) or ASLIB Professional Recruitment Ltd, are more suitable for the recruitment of staff with library and information services skills; the addresses for these organizations are given at the end of the book. Recruitment to senior management posts can also be undertaken by recruitment consultants, who assume responsibility for advertising, initial shortlisting and 'headhunting', so that suitable potential employees are made aware of posts for which they have the right mix of skills. Recruitment consultants can also carry out preliminary screening of shortlisted candidates. Clear and specific written instructions must be given to such consultants and agreement reached with them, before they start work, about the extent of their involvement in the recruitment process.

Whatever method of recruitment is used you will find it useful to keep simple statistics to evaluate the effectiveness of the advertising medium over a period of time. In this way, detailed costs can be measured against the number of applications, and whether those applications were from suitable or unsuitable candidates.

Content of the advertisement

Before drafting any advertisement, take time to look at examples which have already appeared in the journal or newspaper of your choice. This will give you ideas about size, style, approach and content. Some advertisements which use graphics and company logos can be eye-catching: it is worthwhile remembering that any advertisement says a lot about the organization itself. Such graphics can be very effective in communicating messages about the job or the organization, for example, a picture of a black person or a woman in the advertisement signals that applications from people from ethnic minorities, or from both men and women, are welcome. In any case, advertisements should not discriminate on the grounds of race or sex. Specific circumstances where this might be allowed should be checked in the appropriate national legislation. In the UK, this would mean checking the Sex Discrimination Act 1975 and the Race Relations Act 1976. There is particular legislation applicable in Northern Ireland.

Increasingly it is recommended that specific ages should also not appear in the advertisement. The Equal Opportunities Commission [4], have published guidance notes on the Sex Discrimination Act and Advertising which contain a job advertisement checklist to help people compiling advertisements to guard against any bias.

An advertisement should include:

- A short description of the employing organization
- A job title and basic outline of duties
- Job location
- Qualities, qualifications and experience expected of applicants
- Salary range and other benefits
- Details about the post – part-time, job-share, hours etc.
- Instructions about applying for further information and application forms if required
- A closing date with name and address for completed applications

If you are placing the advertisement in a number of journals, with different publication dates, you will need to carefully coordinate the closing date: normally 2–3 weeks from the date of publication is sufficient but this period may need to be extended to take account of publication schedules. If you are likely to have many vacancies it is a good practice to establish a numbering system and to ensure that this reference number is quoted in the advertisement and is written on to all application forms before they are dispatched to prospective candidates.

It can also be useful to give a telephone number and named person for job hunters to contact for more detailed information. If you decide on this course of action, ensure that the telephone is always answered, even if only by an answering machine, so that enquirers can be rung back. Nothing sends out the wrong messages faster than an unanswered telephone or the nominated contact person being unobtainable.

Responding to requests for further information

Information about the vacant post should be prepared together with background information about the parent organization. These information packs, together with a blank application form, duly marked with the job title and advertisement number, can be prepared in envelopes before the advertisement appears. It is then a simple operation to send information to the applicants. Essential information includes:

- The job description
- The conditions of employment – hours, pay scales, annual holiday, health schemes and medical insurance, pension schemes and other benefits.

Additional information can include:

- The mission statement for the organization and the LIS
- Statistical information about the organization and the LIS
- A staff organization chart
- Copies of recent publications, such as annual reports, policy statements etc.

Potential applicants should also be told whether or not their application will be acknowledged, and when it is hoped to hold the interviews.

Application forms

The use of application forms means that all candidates present their information in a standardized format, which makes it easier for the assessors to consider each application and to review and compare one applicant against another. Applications forms generally follow a similar pattern, to include surname or family name, first name(s), date of birth/age, education/qualifications, details of posts held or previous experience, reason for applying for the post and details of referees. If you need to design an application form, you can easily obtain a selection of sample forms by responding to advertisements yourself, although not all of these will necessarily represent good practice. A basic example application form is provided by ACAS [5].

You will need to establish at what stage candidates are willing for references to be taken up – some are reluctant to alert current employers to the fact that they are job hunting, and are only happy for this to happen if they are to be offered the post; to clarify this, a statement can be printed on the application form to the effect that no approach will be made to a current employer unless there is an offer of employment.

Some forms ask for marital status and other personal details which, strictly speaking, are not necessary to the job application; however, forms are sometimes used to monitor recruitment from various special groups, whether by race, gender, age or disability status; this information is usually on a detachable strip that is removed before the selection panel meets. It is common practice in many European countries for a photograph to be requested.

Curricula vitae, although not in a standardized format, can reveal much about a candidate simply by style and what has been included or omitted, and are equally valid as application forms in the selection process. Outside the public sector, letters of application with accompanying CVs are often used in preference to application forms.

Receiving applications

Separate files should be established for each vacancy, headed with the post title and number if used, the vacancy number and the closing date. In case of query, a copy of the advertisement should be kept in the file. You may wish to list the names and addresses of all people requesting further information, but the minimum you should keep is a running total of applications; this will help you assess the success of the advertisement.

As completed applications are received, they should be numbered, listed and filed, and if you are acknowledging receipt this should be done immediately: to keep costs down some employers ask candidates to send in a stamped addressed envelope if they require acknowledgement; this practice is extended much further in Belgium, where candidates for posts in any state institution are required to submit a small fee for every job application they make – this is intended to cover the administration costs of the potential employer and signals the serious interest of the candidate in making the application. In the UK the acknowledgement need only be in the form of a printed card, with details of the post and date of receipt of the application filled in. Applications can be taken up to the end of the closing date, although some employers prefer to wait until receipt of the mail on the following day. You should ensure that applications are not delayed by internal mail processes.

Drawing up a shortlist

If the interview is to be by a panel, completed copies of the applications should be given to every member of the panel, with a time limit in which to draw up their own shortlist – some employers will hold a panel meeting to do this in order to justify and collate different decisions.

Shortlisting should be done by careful evaluation of the applications against the essential minimum criteria in the person specification. No one applicant is going to meet all the criteria listed, but armed with this and the job description it is relatively easy to eliminate those who clearly fail to do so: for example, if a specific qualification is deemed essential it becomes a simple matter to reject all those not holding that qualification. Other factors which need to be considered include presentation and layout of the application, type and duration of previous experience, and grading in examinations (if appropriate). Particularly helpful in shortlisting is any information supplied by the candidate in support of their application – it is this section, especially if it has been geared to the job in question, that can determine the difference between one candidate and another.

There is a limit to the number of people that can be interviewed properly in one day: you should aim for a maximum of eight interviews, although six is more manageable – concentration levels fall and fatigue can set in if you attempt to do more. If you are only interviewing for one post, a much shorter shortlist may be desirable. The whole object of the shortlist is an initial sifting of candidates – it is unnecessary and wasteful of time and money to call all applicants for interview, although in some countries it is official policy to do so for posts connected with government work.

Before drawing up the final shortlist, remember to identify and put into ranked order those applications which might be considered at a later stage. If one of the shortlisted candidates drops out it becomes a straightforward task to contact the next person on this list of 'possibles' without going through the shortlisting procedure again.

Setting up the interview

Interviewing is only one of a possible range of staff selection techniques, and although some employers no longer rely solely on this method, it has consistently remained the most popular. Reasonable notice of the interview must be given to candidates: telephoning to agree an interview date can shortcircuit much paperwork and save time. Interview schedules need not be arranged in any particular order but can take account of distances people have to travel – normally you should allow at least a half to one hour per interview, depending on the complexity of the post and the number of people on the panel; some interviews for senior posts may take much longer. However, all interviews for the same post should be of similar length, scope and format.

It should be policy to ask candidates to confirm their intention to attend the interview, and if there are any internal delays the candidates should be kept informed so that they do not lose interest. In calling candidates to interview it is good practice to advise:

- The date and time of the interview
- The estimated duration of the interview
- The names of and posts held by the interviewers
- Instructions about travel and access to the building
- Information about reimbursement of travel, accommodation and meal expenses, if offered.

If the candidate is not a national of the country or otherwise automatically entitled to work, for example, as a European Community national in any member state, you must ask for documentation proving this right; this information is usually shown in the passport entry stamp or on the visa. To save a great deal of frustration and waste of effort, it is advisable to check this at the time of interview as it may not be possible for an employer to obtain a work permit easily or quickly, if at all.

It has also become standard practice to invite candidates to an informal interview to look over the premises or to tour the building: although not a formal part of the selection process these contacts can be very revealing – more can be gleaned from an unguarded remark or reaction to a situation than may be elicited at interview. In some interviews the candidates are required to make a short presentation, on either a pre-agreed topic or a topic decided on the day of the interview: it is only fair to let candidates know that this will be expected of them.

On the day of the interview, the list of candidates and the interview times should be available to the receptionist or whoever will be the first point of contact; you must also designate a waiting area for candidates – this is a good time for them to complete expenses forms. The interview panel should endeavour to keep closely to the interview times, the setting of which should be realistic and allow for tea/coffee breaks during the day.

Other types of screening and assessment

As well as the interview, employers can use other forms of screening to assess candidates, not just for initial selection but also for promotion, redeployment or counselling:

- The testing of ability and aptitudes has a large and supporting literature. Occupational testing for example, at its most basic, involves timed tests for speed, spelling or letter layout for secretaries, putting materials into alphabetical or numerical sequences for library staff, or testing for special skills such as computing aptitude.
- Psychological or personality testing is a less exact science and usually involves the completion of tests/questionnaires that aim to reveal the strengths and weaknesses of the candidate's personality: for example, is the person a leader or a follower? The identification of a weakness aids the selection process but should not necessarily prevent an appointment: depending on the problem, on-the-job training can help to overcome weaknesses revealed by personality testing. Although the administration and scoring of these tests is relatively straightforward, they should only be administered by accredited testers. Likewise, the interpretation of the results is difficult and complex and should only by undertaken by trained assessors. As stated in *Psychological testing. a manager's guide*, the British, American and Australian Psychological Societies have all published standards for the guidance of their members [6]. This publication by Toplis examines the variety and methods of psychological assessments, and is a useful starting point if you wish to obtain more information on the subject.
- Graphology is being used more frequently in staff selection, but handwriting analysis is not a precise science either. Handwriting may make a statement about a person's frame of mind at the time of writing: it is doubtful whether it can be used to make predictions

about future success or capabilities in a job. Far more important is legibility and the ability to spell correctly.

The interview panel

This should consist of the direct line manager and at least one other person who will be in a supervisory capacity; the practice of one person interviewing on their own is to be avoided if possible. Some interview panels will involve more staff, especially if the post is to be at a senior level. The panel leader will be responsible for introducing the panel members, for controlling the interview and for setting the tone. The overall style of the interview will be affected by the room layout: a formal arrangement is for the interviewers to sit behind a desk or table; a less formal approach is to sit in a circle with no physical barriers between the candidate and the panel. Consideration must be given to the location of the interview room, as interruptions and noise and lighting factors will affect the concentration of both panel and candidates – sitting candidates in the full glare of the sun will not help them perform well.

All interviews need to be carefully planned and the final selection will only be as good as the pre-preparation planning. Ideally, all members of the panel should have had training in interview selection techniques; information about short courses on selection interviewing can be obtained from organizations such as The Library Association, the Institute of Personnel Management or the Industrial Society. The panel should meet before the interview to plan the structure of the interview and decide on the range of questions for each member of the panel to ask.

Setting and asking the questions

The structure of the interview must be clear to all those participating; it seems obvious to state that there must be a beginning, a middle section – in which most of the questioning takes place – and an end sequence. The panel leader should consider a range of opening and closing strategies for the interview; two-way communication, at these times, is important to create a relaxed and constructive atmosphere and to put the nervous candidate at ease.

Two aids in deciding which questions to set are the person

specification and the job description. A study of the application forms will also highlight specific questions arising from the candidates' submissions. Plan the questioning so that it follows a logical sequence of approach. In some organizations it has been policy to ask the same questions of each candidate and to allow for no subsidiary questioning, but this method is particularly unhelpful in assessing future members of staff. It is perfectly in order to have a standard core of questions which you intend to ask of each candidate, but singularly unhelpful and unwise if the answers to those questions cannot be pursued – it is very often at that stage that you begin to analyse the candidate's true potential. During the interview, do not waste time by going through the application form – you already have that information, although it is useful to pick up on specific points which you wish to pursue; what you need now is additional information, particularly about interpersonal skills and personality if these are important to the post. Members of the interview panel should prepare an interview checklist to act as an *aide mémoire* for the salient points to be raised during the interviews. The checklist may include:

- Checks for omissions/gaps on the application form and in the career history
- Checks on educational qualifications and certificates; employers in the UK may be unsure of the relative value of many EC qualifications, even though there is provision for mutual recognition under *The European Communities Recognition of Professional Qualifications Regulations* [7].
- Exploring the candidate's job motivation
- Candidate's reason for applying for the post, and their expectations of the job
- Candidate's interests, awareness, sociability, practical abilities, and any relevant previous experience which would assure a minimum of training – although a positive and enthusiastic personality can sometimes outweigh the lack of experience
- Checks on the candidate's state of health.

Interviewers must attempt to make effective use of questioning techniques; this means no rhetorical questions, no multipart questions and no leading questions. Questions should be probing or open-ended to solicit views and opinions; opening gambits can include questions like 'Tell us about . . .' or 'What is your experience of . . .?' Advanced interviewing skills include having the ability to generate a topic of conversation in order to establish a framework for indirect questioning. This presupposes that the interviewers are actively listening to the candidate's responses to initial questions and are prepared to probe, question or query statements; the process of active listening which includes eye contact and body movement should help, not hinder, the interview.

The interview panel should take note of the non-verbal behaviour of the candidates, which reflects their mental attitude to the selection process: attitude at interview is as vital to the selection criteria as is the ability to think clearly and lucidly. If the candidate is from another country, their ability to read, write and speak fluently in English is essential if they are to be productive from the onset of employment; however technical terms can always be picked up quickly by a person who is really fluent in a language.

Depending on the level of the post, and if the information has not already been provided, it would be helpful to tell a candidate at interview:

- The job content
- Basic conditions of employment, such as the hours of work, holiday entitlement etc.
- Any staff benefits such as health plans, pensions plans, parking, meal vouchers etc.
- Method and frequency of salary payments
- The probationary period procedures
- The processes following the interview and when and how they will be informed of the outcome.

At the end of the interview time should be allowed for the candidate to ask questions; this can be a good time to clarify points relating to conditions of service. At this stage candidates may be introduced to members of the department, if a tour has not already taken place.

Interview documentation

It is essential for each member of the panel to keep accurate notes of the interview. Some organizations have formal job interview sheets, which are prepared in advance and attached to each interviewee's documentation. Some interview sheets contain headings under which the interviewers record their impressions – personal impact, presentation and articulation, alertness, disposition, motivation and attitude. Other attributes needed for the job can be gleaned from the person speci-fication: these can be further defined as either essential or desirable for the job. The advantage of interview sheets is that they are a useful and practical aid to the fair assessment of the candidates, as they ensure that comparisons between the candidates' performance at interview can be measured accurately, instead of relying on memory, when the panel comes to evaluate all the information. It is important that the selection panel are clear about their reasons for rejecting or selecting a candidate; these reasons should be recorded on the interview sheets. Completion of the interview sheets needs to be done discreetly while maintaining rapport with the candidate.

Interview sheets must be signed and dated by each interviewer at the end of the selection process. The sheets can be produced at any sub-sequent enquiry and are especially useful if the selection processes are challenged by a candidate who feels they have been discriminated against. The interview sheets should be stapled to the application forms and kept in the job file. It is important to establish a retention and disposal policy and to store these confidential papers in a secure place. It is usual to store unsuccessful applications for about 12 months.

Offering the post

It should be noted that even a verbal offer of a post is legal in the UK. It is quicker to telephone, as this lets the candidates know exactly where they stand, but some people only telephone the successful candidate to confirm that they are willing to accept the post – the unsuccessful candidates are sent letters. Whatever procedure is adopted it is essential that all candidates are told of the result. If you intend to telephone, check where and when the candidates can be contacted. When offering a post at this stage, specify, both verbally and in writing, that the offer is subject to satisfactory references and medical clearance.

If your first choice either refuses or requests more time, or attempts to negotiate different conditions that you may not be able to meet, it is prudent to have a second reserve to whom you can offer the post; if this is the case do not contact this person until you are certain that your first choice has either accepted or rejected the offer. In any case, set a time limit for your first choice to come back to you with a firm decision. Any telephone offer should be followed up as soon as possible with written details of the offer of appointment, including details of salary.

Once a candidate has had an offer of a post and accepted it they acquire contractual rights from the time of acceptance, even if they have not yet started work. If for any reason you were unable to continue with the offer of the job, the person would be entitled to pursue any grievance, disciplinary or redundancy procedures which applied to them in their contract.

The purpose of the reference

You should be aware of subjective bias in references which can work to the benefit or the detriment of the candidate. If you request the reference before interview, the experienced interviewer will look for what has been left unsaid: this may highlight possible questions at interview, or reinforce impressions already formed. You should know what information you want and expect to have supplied in a reference. The purpose of the reference is to:

- Verify some of the candidate's information, such as posts held, dates employed, salary earned
- Obtain information about the candidate's past work performance
- Elicit the referee's opinion of the candidate's suitability for the post
- Answer any specific questions you may have asked, e.g. about attendance and health records.

You should advise any potential employee not to resign from their current post until you have cleared their references and medical examination. It is usual to have at least two referees, at least one of whom should be a previous employer. It is advisable to contact a current employer even if they are not listed for the testimonial purposes – if you intend to do this, you should ask the candidate if this is acceptable; in the private sector this should only be done with the candidate's agreement, as otherwise their continued career prospects with that employer could be jeopardized if you ultimately fail to confirm the offer of the post. You should also advise the referee whether or not the reference will be in confidence, as it is now quite common for employers to allow the candidate access to it; if this is the case you may find the reference is extremely circumspect. Telephoning can result in a more informal and direct response but will need the support of a written reference. It is important to send the referees details of the job on offer, so that they can relate the candidate's qualities to a specific job.

Sending the letter of appointment

It is good practice to send the letter of appointment immediately you have cleared the candidate as suitable for employment; this letter should include a statement of the terms of employment. Under Section 1 of the Employment Protection (Consolidation) Act 1978, all employers in the UK are required to do this not later than within 13 weeks of the employee starting work. This should include:

- Basic facts about the post, e.g. name and address of the employer, job title, grade, whether permanent or part-time, and location.
- Exact salary and dates of any increments, pension scheme if appropriate, and how salary will be paid.
- Conditions of employment – commencement date, hours, shift work, holiday entitlement, medical or sick pay schemes.
- Period of probation and notice required from both sides to terminate the post.

Since this is a legal document, new staff should be asked to return a signed copy, which must be kept on their personnel file. If you operate a performance appraisal scheme, details of this must appear in the letter or contract of employment.

New staff also need to be briefed about what to do on their arrival at work on the first day, and about the documents they need to bring with them. Staff need to know:

- Where to report and at what time
- Location of staff entrance and any admission formalities, such as the need for an identity card or letter
- The name of their line manager
- Hours of duty for the first week or two.

They will also need information about booking holidays, sick leave notification and procedures, medical coverage, and the grievance procedure, although this need not necessarily be provided at this stage; the usual practice is to cover these points during the induction process.

New staff may need to bring with them:

- Birth/marriage certificates (required for pension schemes)
- National Insurance number in the UK
- Details of their previous salary taxation
- Details of previous pension schemes, if appropriate.

Staff may expect the following statutory salary deductions:

- Tax. In the UK this is deducted by a PAYE scheme (pay as you earn). The employer informs the Inland Revenue when a new member of staff starts work and the employee will receive a tax return to complete; this enables the tax authorities to notify the employer of how much tax to deduct from the salary: if the form is not completed the employee may well end up paying a far higher emergency tax than they need. Staff should be reminded to claim tax relief on their professional subscriptions. You can obtain all the necessary forms from a local tax office.
- National Insurance. Deductions are earnings-related and are important because they enable the employee to receive state sickness benefit, state unemployment benefit and the state old-age pension. Employees can also pay into SERPS (state earnings-related pension scheme) or can opt out of SERPS to either join an employer's pension fund or a free-standing pension scheme. A good employer, although not involved in the decision, should ensure that employees are aware of all the pension options available to them.

An example of excellent practice in recruitment and selection procedures comes from The Hague, in the Netherlands. Here a selection code [8] considers the process of a job application from the point of view of the applicant. Starting from the concept that 'the applicant is also a human being', this detailed code outlines the rights of the applicant to information, privacy, confidential treatment and proper and prompt procedures, and gives notice of their right to complain and how to complain if unfairly treated. The interview procedures are explained in detail, including timescales. Bearing in mind the right to privacy, the code states that information concerning the applicant can only be obtained from a previous employer if the applicant agrees, and, interestingly, the results of any psychological testing go initially to the candidate, who has the right to discuss the report with the psychologist and the right to prevent the report being given to the prospective employer. A further example of good practice comes from the personnel department of the City of Newcastle upon Tyne. The aim of their code of practice [9] is to assist those involved in recruitment and selection procedures to carry out those procedures in a fair, efficient and cost-effective manner. The code takes the member of staff through a step-by-step procedure for filling a vacancy, including writing the job description and the person specification. Advice and guidance are given about methods of recruitment, wording of advertisements, the treatment of applications and the conduct of the interview. As with the selection code used in The Hague, the complaints procedure for candidates who feel they have been unlawfully discriminated against, is explained in detail. The applicant's right to complain is also explained on the application form.

Ensuring equality of opportunity

Over the past few years there have been major changes in attitudes to and perceptions of equal opportunities in employment and training. This has come about partly by the passing of legislation aimed at eliminating discrimination and promoting equal opportunities. However, there is a difference between taking positive action – and positive discrimination, which can be termed reverse discrimination and is unlawful – and the exercising of a non-discriminatory policy.

Employing people with disabilities

The Americans with Disabilities Act, whose employment clauses apply from 1992, makes an employer liable to civil action if they discriminate against a person on the grounds of disability or because they associate with someone who has a disability: disability is defined as a physical or mental impairment which constitutes a substantial limitation to major life activity. The Act will affect the selection, promotion and dismissal rights of employees. Under this Act, employers will be required to provide reasonable accommodation for anyone who is qualified to perform the essential functions of the job and covered by the Act – this means widening doors and building ramps for wheelchairs, and providing flexible shift patterns. Employers will also be liable to civil action if they try to segregate work to be done by people with disabilities; at the same time, they are required to allocate tasks in a way which will make it easier for people with disabilities to perform them.

So far there is no such legislation in force in the UK. The Disabled Persons (Employment) Acts 1944 and 1958 set up the disabled persons register. This is a voluntary register for people who, although substantially handicapped because of a disability, have reasonable prospects of obtaining and keeping a job, and want to be in paid employment or to work for themselves. The Disabled Persons (Employment) Act 1944 also established a quota system by which employers with 20 or more employees have a duty to employ registered disabled people as 3% of their total workforce; it is not an offence to be below this quota, providing a permit is obtained from the Employment Service Disablement Resettlement Officer. The permit is issued on two conditions:

1. That all vacancies are notified to the Job Centre and the Disablement Resettlement Officer
2. That the employer is willing to consider sympathetically the recruitment of people with disabilities who are qualified to apply for vacancies.

The legislation also allows for a designated employment scheme under which certain occupations are reserved for people with disabilities – these posts, such as a car-park attendant or a passenger lift attendant, do not count towards filling an employer's quota if they are occupied by registered disabled people.

Cash grants are available in the UK to enable modifications to offices and equipment, and job introduction schemes allow people with disabilities to be taken on a trial basis. There are also other types of financial and practical assistance for the employment and training of people with disabilities. Detailed information on these can be obtained from the appropriate government employment department.

All companies employing, on average, more than 250 staff, must conform to that part of the Companies Act 1985 concerning policy statements about the employment and training of people with disabilities. Such companies are required to include in the directors' report of the Annual Report and Accounts, a statement describing what policy the company has operated in the past year towards the recruitment and career development of people with disabilities.

As discussed in Chapter 1, employers who are subject to the quota system, or who have designated employments, are required to keep records, for 2 years from the period to which they relate, showing:

- The names of all people employed, with start and end dates, including those not working full-time
- Lists of registered disabled employees (including those whose registration has lapsed while employed)
- Staff employed under a work permit
- Staff employed in designated employment for disabled people, such as car-park attendants.

These records must be made available for inspection, if so required, by officials from the Employment Service of the Department of Employment.

The *Code of good practice on the employment of disabled people* [10] published by the Employment Service in England, Wales and Scotland and the Department of Economic Development in Northern Ireland, is a useful but voluntary guide for employers who wish to establish a policy of positive and effective practices in the employment and training of people with disabilities.

Racial and sexual discrimination in employment

Major legislation in the UK affecting equality of opportunity is:

1. The Race Relations Act 1976, valid in the UK (except in Northern Ireland where separate legislation applies). Discrimination under this Act would be on the grounds of colour, race, nationality and other ethnic or national origins.
2. The Sex Discrimination Act 1975, covering discrimination on the grounds of sex and marital status. It refers to men as well as women.
3. The Equal Pay Act 1970, affecting claims for equal pay for work of equal value. This has been discussed in Chapter 1.

Under the Race Relations Act and the Sex Discrimination Act, Commissions were established to:

- Work towards the elimination of discrimination
- Promote equality of opportunity
- Review the workings of the Acts and propose amendments
- Issue codes of practice whose objectives are to promote equal opportunities and eliminate discrimination in employment.

The Commission for Racial Equality and the Equal Opportunities Commission can conduct formal investigations in relation to these duties, and can recommend changes in practices or procedures to promote equality of opportunity. As a result of these formal investigations the Commissions can also serve non-discrimination notices on employers: failure to comply with a notice means that the employer can be taken to court to have the order enforced.

According to the Acts there are three specific types of discrimination:

1. Direct discrimination – treating a person less favourably because of their race or sex
2. Indirect discrimination – this could mean that an employer has instituted a requirement which, although not intentional, adversely affects people of a certain racial group or sex
3. Victimization – those who provide information about alleged contravention of the Acts are protected from discrimination

These Acts provide staff and applicants for posts with statutory rights for which they need neither a contract of employment nor a period of service. Claims of racial or sexual discrimination, for example, can be made by applicants for posts during any of the selection procedures.

Complaints are dealt with by industrial tribunals, with the burden of proof being on the complainant. If the tribunal finds in favour of the complainant it can issue:

- An order declaring the rights of parties; this is used when the complainant has had rights violated but suffered no actual loss
- An order for the employer to pay compensation, which covers damages such as injured feelings
- A recommendation for the employer to take a specific course of action.

Such rights are by no means limited to the UK. For example, in the USA the Federal Anti-Discrimination Laws, Title V11 of the Civil Rights Act 1964, covers discrimination in employment on the basis of sex, colour, race, religion and national origin. The federal agency responsible for enforcing Title V11 is the Equal Employment Opportunity Commission, which was one of the first organizations to recognize that sexual harassment is a form of sex discrimination at work; this is now supported by a ruling of the Supreme Court of the United States in 1986, that a claim can be brought under the Civil Rights Act 1964 if a hostile or offensive working environment exists. The American Library Association Committee on the Status of Women in Librarianship has produced a useful leaflet defining sexual harassment at work and its effects, and offering advice and guidelines about what to do to resolve it [11]. The EC has produced a draft code of practice to help employers and employees develop policies to effectively deal with sexual harassment. This is accompanied by printed proposals on the protection of the dignity of men and women at work. The recommendations urge member states to promote awareness that sexual discrimination is unacceptable and can constitute an infringement of the EC Equal Treatment Directive. The Library Association also provides policy statements on a variety of issues concerning equal opportunities and employment in LIS work. These policy statements, which are issued in the form of an equal opportunities pack, are available from the Employment and Resources Department of the Library Association.

The Equal Opportunities Commission publish *Guidelines for Equal Opportunities Employers* [12] in which they outline ten essential steps to becoming an equal opportunities employer. Model guidance notes are included for interviewers, and advice on the design of application forms so that they are free of bias. A section on monitoring an equal opportunity policy is included – it is important to ensure that any information so gathered is used to ensure the effectiveness of the equal opportunities policy, and never used at any stage in the staff selection procedures, as to do so could give rise to a complaint of unlawful discrimination.

Discrimination on the grounds of age

Organizations should review their policies to prevent the inadvertent or inappropriate use of age in employment decisions, since decisions taken on age-related criteria are ineffective and reduce objectivity. Age discrimination takes place not just at the recruitment stage but also in decisions over training, career development, promotions and retirement, and this can have an adverse effect on the delivery of the service to the customer. For example, the full effect of the disproportionate number of older and experienced library staff taking early retirement over the past few years has yet to be assessed. Retaining older people on the workforce may mean taking decisions on flexible working or reduced working hours, and not being affected by the stereotype of the the older person who is slow to learn or adapt to new procedures –

which of course is not true. The current UK position is that the workforce itself is ageing, and although the government believes that discrimination on the grounds of age undermines effective human resource planning, it prefers to tackle age discrimination by persuasion and education. Recommendations for reducing age discrimination in employment appear in the IPM Statement *Age and employment* [13]. In the USA the Age Discrimination in Employment Act has been in force for more than 20 years, and similar legislation is in place in many European countries.

An example of good practice of a library policy statement concerning equal opportunities is given below, with the kind permission of the Queens Borough Public Library, New York.

Policy and Procedure Manual

Equal Employment Opportunity Program
POLICY (issued November 1989)

The Queens Borough Public Library reaffirms its determination to comply with City, State and Federal anti-discrimination laws as they relate to employment in this library, consistent with the concept of merit in employment

The policy of the Equal Employment Opportunity Program (EEOP) and the procedure of handling informal complaints reflects this library's attitude and its intention to:

1. Review all aspects of employment policies and practices as they relate to recruitment, hiring, promotion, transfer, disciplinary procedures, separations, benefits, library sponsored training, educational assistance and other terms and conditions of employment.

2. Determine whether any of the above policies and practices have resulted in an adverse impact on minorities and/or the disabled and are preventing such groups from entry into or advancement in employment in accordance with their skill and ability.

3. Insure that all personnel actions are administered without regard to race, creed, color, religion, sex, age or national origin, disability, marital status or sexual orientation and that all

employment decisions are made so as to further the principles of equal opportunity.

4. Provide, pursuant to the Vocational Rehabilitation Act of 1973, equal employment opportunity as set forth above to qualified disabled or handicapped persons.

This Library will make copies of this Policy and Procedure available to employees and applicants. The Executive Assistant to the Director shall be designated as the EEO Officer for the Library. He/she has the overall responsibility for the establishment and implementation of the EEOP which also includes working with other personnel in:

1. Internal and external communications of EEOP provisions.

2. Identifying problem areas and assisting supervisors to solve those problems as they arise.

3. Implementing audit and reporting systems which will:

   (a) measure effectiveness of the program and
   (b) indicate need for remedial action.

4. Serving as liaison between the Library, the City Commission on Human Rights, minority and women's organizations and community actions groups concerned with the employment opportunities for minorities, women and other covered groups.

5. Conducting quarterly and annual audits of hiring and promotion patterns to aid in the advancement of the objectives of the EEOP

Policy statements

You should consider drafting an equal opportunities policy which clearly states a commitment not to discriminate on the grounds of race, sex, gender, ability, age, colour, ethnic or national origin, marital status or sexual orientation. The above example deals with the library's willingness to tackle discrimination issues in all aspects of its employment practices and policies, including training. An important point to note is that clear responsibility for the policy is allocated to a senior member of staff; this direct and specific responsibility ensures the success of the programme.

EC directives and recommendations

It is important to be aware of the EC dimension in human resource management. European regulations and directives are legally binding on member states, although the method of implementing directives is left to those states; this is the case with the Directive on Display Screen Equipment, discussed in Chapter 6.

Recommendations, resolutions and declarations are not legally binding but can be used to interpret or support national law. Europe-wide social policy amendments, also known as the Social Chapter, were agreed at the Maastricht Summit Agreement in 1991, by all the member states except the UK. Among other provisions these amendments call for Europe-wide provisions for 14 weeks' paid maternity leave for pregnant women, improved terms and conditions of employment for part-time and temporary workers, guaranteeing them the same rights as full-time staff on a pro rata basis, and proposals on equal opportunities. At the time of writing, none of these later amendments have been adopted by the UK. Pertinent and up-to-date information about EC legislation is available in *The single European market and personnel management* [14]. A further publication which explores the impact of employment legislation at EC level within the human resource context is *Employment and Training* [15] published by Mercury books in association with the Confederation of British Industry Initiative 1992.

References

1. Rodger, Alec (1952) *The seven-point plan*. National Institute of Industrial Psychology
2. Rawling, K. (1985) *The seven-point plan: new perspectives fifty years on*. Windsor: NFER-Nelson
3. Bolton, G. M. (1983) *Interviewing for selection decisions*. Windsor: NFER-Nelson
4. Equal Opportunities Commission (1991) *The Sex Discrimination Act and Advertising: guidance notes*. Manchester: EOC
5. Advisory, Conciliation and Arbitration Service (1990) *Employing people: the ACAS handbook for small firms*. London: ACAS
6. Toplis, John *et al.* (1991) *Psychological testing: a manager's guide*, 2nd ed. London: IPM
7. *The European Communities Recognition of Professional Qualifications Regulations; Statutory Instrument No 824* (1991) London: HMSO
8. Gemeente Den Haag (1990)*Sollicitatiecode*. The Hague
9. City of Newcastle upon Tyne (1992) *Code of practice on Recruitment and Selection*. City of Newcastle upon Tyne: Personnel Dept.
10. Employment Service (1990) *Code of good practice on the employment of disabled people*. London: Employment Department Group

11. American Library Association (1988) *Sexual harassment in the workplace*. Committee on the Status of Women in Librarianship. Chicago: ALA

12. Equal Opportunities Commission (1980) *Guidelines for equal opportunities employers*. Manchester: EOC

13. Institute of Personnel Management (1991) *Age and employment: an IPM statement*. London: IPM

14. Mill, Cherry (1991) *The single European market and personnel management*. London: Institute of Personnel Management

15. Manpower PLC (1990) *Employment and training*. London: Mercury Books

CHAPTER THREE

Performance appraisal and reward

One of the earliest and most essential forms of staff appraisal is the assessment of a new member of staff during their period of probation. The contract of employment will have outlined the exact timescale of the probation period: usually 6 months is adequate to decide whether or not a person is suitable to be retained on the permanent staff.

The purpose of the probation period

The assessment of staff on probation is quite different from assessing and appraising permanent staff. The main purpose is to decide if the probationer is good enough to retain on the permanent staff, or whether a mistake has been made, in that the person has failed in practice to fit the requirements of the organization. This critical decision requires absolute objectivity from the library's point of view. It is usual for a person on probation to be formally assessed about half-way through their probation period and again at the end of the period – say at 3 months and then just before the end of 6 months – although no one should wait for these periods of time to elapse before tackling the problem of a member of staff who is patently not fulfilling the requirements of the post.

Induction training, as discussed in Part Two of this book, will form an important part of the probation period. If a probationer has been given adequate induction training and they are adapting well, then the initial assessment will be one of encouragement for their performance so far; if performance is inadequate or they are in any other way unsatisfactory, then these points must be examined and discussed. Further training may be provided if necessary, but the probationer must be left in no doubt about what will happen at the end of the probation period if they do not improve. Any decisions taken by you at the probation interviews must be confirmed in writing, outlining the likely outcome if no improvement is forthcoming. Barraclough and Nilsson in *Ready drafted employment letters* [1] give examples of such letters, which can be adapted to suit particular circumstances.

If at the end of the period the probationer is still deemed to be unsuitable, then you are perfectly within your rights to dismiss them from the staff with due period of notice, as in their contract of employment. In the UK dismissal can take place within the first 24 months without the member of staff being able to claim unfair dismissal and seek redress from an industrial tribunal. However, you should always ensure that the dismissal is fair and that your procedures leading up to the dismissal are reasonable and well documented. Whatever the legal position, dismissing a member of staff is never an easy task but, however distasteful, dismissal is far easier in the long run than retaining an unsuitable member of staff who, once made permanent, will absorb more staff time and energy than you can possibly imagine, and who can have a negative impact on both the service and other staff.

Terminating someone's employment need not be an entirely negative process: being unsuitable for one type of job does not mean that the probationer will be unsuitable for other employment, and you may be able to suggest other areas of work better suited to their abilities. If you are terminating the employment of a probationer you may like to give them the option of resigning rather than being dismissed. This course of action has definite advantages from the point of view of their seeking future employment, but disadvantages if they need to claim unemployment benefit, since anyone who makes themselves intentionally unemployed in the UK cannot claim this benefit for 26 weeks. A probationer who is leaving your service may also want to know if you will supply a reference on their behalf to any future employer; you must clarify in your own mind the extent to which you will be able to respond favourably to any such request. You are under no obligation to provide a future character reference; organizational policy can also influence your ability to do so.

There are rare occasions when the period of probation should be extended – for instance, when a person has suffered a bereavement, which understandably may affect performance at work. In such a case you may wish to give the probationer longer to adjust to the job before reaching a final decision; you should interview the probationer and tell them exactly what you propose to do, and again confirm that decision in writing. If at the end of the probation period you decide to retain the probationer, a letter confirming that decision is equally necessary.

Performance appraisal systems

Apart from probation appraisals, which have a specific objective, informal staff appraisals happen all the time – most people in supervisory posts form opinions about their staff, but very often these opinions may not be objective, nor discussed with the employee. This is unfair, since the employee being judged may not know the criteria on which that judgement is based. Neither is it satisfactory for an appraisal to work in one way only – appraisals should be used as a way of communicating between supervisors and their staff. Staff appraisal is increasingly recognized as an important component in employee relations; better communications leads to improved staff motivation and this in turn leads to better service for the library user.

There is a confusing array of different appraisal schemes currently in use under the guise of performance management, including total quality management and performance appraisal, which may or may not be linked to pay. Despite this diversity of approach, most good appraisal schemes have a common core in that they evaluate staff performance, set goals and objectives, examine training needs and praise and reward achieved objectives. Most schemes can be both retrospective and forward-looking at the same time, in that they review past performance and set objectives for the future. An extremely helpful introductory booklet produced by ACAS *Employee appraisal*[2] contains practical examples of appraisal forms and is a good starting point if you wish to design an appraisal system. The case studies in Part Two of this book look in detail at particular schemes which operate within the LIS environment.

The American Library Association [3] has issued a practical guide for library staff who are introducing performance appraisal. This includes guidelines for formulating individual performance goals and a bibliography on the performance appraisal, compiled from library and business literature.

The evaluation and rewarding of LIS staff performance is an essential activity of management, but the method should be carefully considered. Rewards do not necessarily have to be financial, and reward-driven schemes which measure staff performance currently represent only one type of performance management; the other type of scheme is development-driven. Some reward systems may even frustrate any training and development processes present in development-driven schemes. A recent major survey conducted by the Institute of Personnel Management [4] found that too much emphasis on pay at the expense of development could lead to disillusionment with performance management, and that some performance-related pay systems, designed to increase staff achievements, were in fact divisive and demotivating for the majority of the staff involved. The survey, albeit not conducted in libraries, did not find any clear indication that pay by performance, for example, actually increased job satisfaction to the required level. Thus great care must be taken when deciding on the type and form of performance appraisal system you wish to introduce into the library.

Performance management

Performance appraisal must be assigned a high priority to reflect its importance for the development of both the organization and the individual. Failure to consider long-term organizational objectives when creating a performance appraisal scheme will ultimately lead to problems, since a performance appraisal system cannot work effectively without a sense of direction.

Performance planning increases the opportunity to achieve objectives by focusing on both the individual and the LIS objectives. The advantage of a performance appraisal system for the line manager is that such a scheme helps to clarify the links between a job and the objectives of the service; although it may not always be easy to incorporate organizational objectives with individual goals, a balance should be maintained between the needs of the organization and the needs of the member of staff. For an employee the advantages are that they obtain a clear view of their job and its place in the organization; performance appraisal should also provide a framework for personal and professional development in which active support and encouragement is received.

It is important to remember that individual appraisal systems and performance-related pay introduced in a vacuum are not necessarily the best way to achieve library objectives, nor to ensure better motivated or more committed staff. Total performance management, used to support total quality management, involves a more integrated approach and has the following broad-based goals:

- To improve the effectiveness of the library
- To manage the salary and wages budget
- To link pay to performance
- To improve and target training and development.

Such a totally integrated system can be used to produce a change in organizational behaviour and the organizational culture.

Integral parts of a forward plan to ensure organizational development include:

- Strong organizational objectives, such as the LIS mission statement or the LIS business plan, which is known to all members of staff.
- Firm but flexible targets for the library which relate to individual goals for members of staff; staff should assist in formulating these targets and goals for their specific area of work.
- Coaching and counselling of staff by regular and formal reviews of these objectives. Coaching indicates a concern to improve performance by training or discussion.

As the objectives of the organization change, it becomes important to evaluate the effectiveness of the entire process and its contribution to the overall effectiveness of LIS organization. Regular reviewing of progress towards set objectives will ensure high standards of staff performance; regular reviews of the practical operation must also take place to maintain commitment and effective implementation of the scheme.

Other important objectives of a performance management scheme would include the following:

- To ensure that line managers take managerial control of their staff and provide effective training and development opportunities
- To improve organizational management by identifying and utilizing the potential of all full-time and part-time staff
- To establish personnel data to improve management decisions on such matters as promotions, transfers or secondments

- To motivate, attract, retain and involve staff
- To improve and target staff performance.

Personnel performance appraisal – a guide for libraries [3] records that a programme of performance appraisal may be considered successful if it has contributed to a greater mutual understanding of responsibilities between the line manager and the member of staff.

The organization of a performance appraisal scheme

Formal staff appraisal schemes should operate on a regular implementation timetable, usually on an annual or biannual basis; on the whole, more frequent appraisals are more satisfactory for staff relations and for the better management of projects. They ensure that the line manager has a more effective oversight of staff operations, and allow for intervention to resolve work situations before they develop into major problems. In any case, it is important to give and collect feedback about progress in achieving any objectives throughout the year, even if this is done informally.

Appraisal techniques include:

- Working to agreed objectives
- A rating system, rating the employee's performance on a scale of about five points from poor to excellent
- Critical incidents; appraising positive and negative behaviour during the period under review
- Narrative reports: these are sometimes additionally linked to a rating system.

The paperwork associated with performance appraisal interviews should be kept as simple as possible, but appraisal forms can include sections for:

- An outline of current job responsibilities
- The objectives of the post
- Targets for the appraisal period
- Methods of achieving these targets
- Training and development agreed for the future
- An agreed timescale for future action
- A progress report for the period under review

- Constraints that may have hindered the achievement of targets
- Comments by the member of staff
- A note of any disagreement
- The signature of the line manager and the member of staff.

All schemes require proper back-up administration, with a trigger system to remind people when appraisals are due. In a small organization this may simply be a diary entry; larger organizations may need a more formal reminder system, such as monthly lists of appraisals due, issued from the personnel department to line managers, or a system of flagging may be built into any computer-based personnel system. All performance appraisal documents are confidential and should not be left lying around. The original record of the performance appraisal should ultimately be filed in the personnel file of the member of staff concerned. Proper procedures for the disposal of confidential material from appraisal documentation must form part of any performance appraisal policy statement.

An essential element of performance appraisal is feedback to the person responsible for arranging staff training and for preparing the training budget; under performance appraisal systems, estimates for training requirements can be directly targeted to known needs.

Training for performance appraisal systems

Special training must be provided for all staff who participate in performance appraisal so that they fully understand the purpose of the scheme, their role and how appraisal will affect their working life. For managerial staff this means:

- Thorough briefing about the objectives of the scheme
- Information about how these objectives can be achieved
- Understanding the mechanics/documentation of the system
- Training in conducting a performance appraisal interview
- Training in review techniques, coaching and counselling

Since inappropriate managerial behaviour can act as a barrier, it is essential that proper resources are assigned for such training. The interviewer will need to develop skills appropriate to conducting a performance appraisal interview, to promote effective review, to listen and to be able to accept feedback and to effectively plan the future performance of their staff. In large organizations the effective and fair operation of any such scheme will rely upon a uniform approach by line managers in deciding how staff will be assessed. This is well illustrated by the Employee Assessment and Development Scheme of Glasgow City Libraries, used as a case study in Part Two. Training packages, such as those produced by the Industrial Society [5], are available to help develop effective skills in conducting appraisal interviews.

For non-supervisory staff, training must include a clear briefing on the objectives and operation of the performance appraisal scheme. They will need to know how the scheme will affect them personally and be familiar with the documentation, the implementation details – such as the timetabling of interviews – and their ultimate right of appeal.

Preparing for a performance appraisal interview

Normally the best person to conduct an appraisal interview is the direct line manager. This is the person who is familiar with the work of the employee and usually assigns and checks it. Most schemes involve the completion of an appraisal form, a copy of which is then given to the employee at an agreed time before the interview date. In some cases a preliminary interview or an informal discussion is arranged, to agree the agenda of the main interview and to allow each party to have time to think about the points they may wish to make. Input, in the form of self-appraisal by the employee, can also form part of this preliminary stage. A relevant point about self-appraisal, made by Glynis Breakwell in *Interviewing* [6], is that if self-appraisal does take place you will need to be aware that many people tend to underplay success and overemphasize failure; as an appraisal interviewer you will need to bear this in mind.

The interview itself should actually contain no surprises; the line manager is simply not managing effectively if problems surface for the first time during an appraisal interview. Any real problems should have been identified during the course of the previous year and resolved as part of the normal reviewing process.

The appraisal of a member of staff should never been be seen as a routine event. It is vital that the line manager spends some time before the interview in reviewing and preparing for it. Familiarity with the past history of the post-holder cannot be avoided and indeed can be useful; however, the line manager must try to remain objective when writing the appraisal report, or at the interview. Likewise, the person being appraised should be encouraged to spend some time putting their own thoughts in order.

Conducting a performance appraisal interview

As with selection interview it is important to ensure access to a comfortable room free from interruptions and noise; as all interviews cause some stress you should try to create a relaxed atmosphere. Since this interview is about the other person, you should be seen to concentrate on them; for example, try to maintain eye contact for at least 70% of the time, and make sure that your face expresses interest in what is being said. It is important to use positive body language by positioning yourself towards the other person and using such techniques as nodding regularly to encourage the appraisee. Awareness of the interviewee's possible nervousness is essential, as are good listening skills.

At the beginning of the interview the line manager should explain how the interview will be conducted and emphasize the need for joint discussion. All the major points that need to be reviewed should be summarized; the structure of the form can be used to structure the interview. The appraisal should focus on achievements rather than personal qualities, and provide an opportunity to discuss with the member of staff the performance of their job against agreed standards and objectives. During the interview the manager should review past performance and any factors that have helped or hindered the achievement of targets. Although the member of staff should always be encouraged to express and record their views, the manager should control the interview by guiding it so that it covers all of the work in the period under review; it is too easy to get side-tracked with one issue, or to just examine recent work. Interviewing techniques as discussed in Chapter 2 will also be useful in the appraisal interview. Further guidance can be obtained from Lawson's *Appraisal and appraisal interviewing* [7].

Ending the performance appraisal interview

All participants must have a clear understanding of the outcome of the interview and the commitment of the member of staff be obtained to pursue all agreed objectives and targets. Having looked at ways of resolving problems and identified barriers to improving performance, the line manager must bring the interview to an end by summarizing agreed action to be taken by both parties. It is important not to make promises that you will not be able to keep – if you are unsure about something it is better to say that you will find out, and let the member of staff have a decision as soon as possible. Only a few important objectives should be agreed, and each should have clear criteria against which to review achievement in the future period. In addition, any learning and training needs should be agreed – this in turn provides data for planning the library training policy and budget. A clearly understandable action plan and future objectives should have been compiled by the end of the interview, and the manager should then ensure that any follow-up action is carried out.

The appraisal interview form, duly signed, is actually a working document and the line manager needs to be able to access it as required; such reports are normally kept in the personnel files until needed. The member of staff also needs a copy of the final document to refer to throughout the year. In some cases the head of department should also see the report before it is filed. A policy decision should be taken on how long these reports should be retained once they are no longer 'live': normally 3 years should be adequate, but this will depend on organizational policy.

Appeals system

In any performance appraisal scheme there should be an integrated appeals system so that an appraisee who feels dissatisfied with the outcome of an interview can seek to have the appraisal or the points of contention reviewed by a more senior member of staff. If necessary, staff should be able to pursue an agreed grievance procedure.

Dealing with a problematic interview

Line managers are generally not averse to evaluating a satisfactory member of staff; they find it more difficult to deal with less satisfactory staff and need to develop the appropriate skills to resolve problematic situations. At an appraisal interview, the employee will have already had access to the appraisal report and probably a pre-interview discussion; they therefore know what points are going to be addressed and have had the opportunity to prepare any response.

At the interview it would be wise to avoid delaying too long before discussing any problem areas. If you have prepared yourself properly for the interview you will be able to anticipate what will be said and how you will deal with it, although it is important to actually listen to what the member of staff is saying. Ensure that you can justify any criticism that you make: total conflict at an interview must be avoided; remember that the purpose of the interview is to resolve the problem. In order to be scrupulously fair, if facts are in dispute agreement should be reached to investigate these and to rearrange the interview for another date, although there will come a time when the manager must simply remain firm about a point of disagreement, and for this reason it is important to be absolutely sure of your facts. Above all, avoid cross-comparison with other staff and steer the discussion away from comments about other staff; after all, the appraisal interview is about the performance of one particular member of staff only.

Bear in mind that in analysing a member of staff you must give due consideration to any constraints that may have affected performance. You must therefore be prepared to discuss work results and difficulties, but point to areas for improvement and ways in which these improvements can be made, which may include arranging some training. Agreeing or setting a timescale for improvements is a positive way forward. Any such problematic member of staff will probably need very careful supervision and regular reviewing to ensure that the targets are being met.

Performance-related pay

Until recently, many public-sector organizations used salary scales on which every member of staff progressed automatically on an annual basis, until they reached the top of the scale; further progression was then dependent on promotion to the next grade or to a higher-graded vacancy. Although in theory it is possible not to award one of these automatic annual increments, the only way to do this is through a disciplinary procedure, the onus of proof of non-performance being on the employer. This is rarely done and is a cumbersome procedure, especially if there is no formal appraisal system in operation. Many employers also regard this automatic right to receive increments as unreasonable, since staff receive a pay increment regardless of performance or ability.

Many libraries now operate pay-by-performance, at least for the most senior posts. The reality that library staff need to be constantly evaluated is now accepted, although at this stage pay-by-performance does not generally apply to lower-graded staff. The objective of performance-related pay is to provide a well-paid, highly motivated workforce geared to the successful achievement of key tasks; the tendency has been to move away from pay scales reached by collective bargaining to the use of personal contracts, which are aimed at improving flexibility and productivity. The theory of performance-related pay and its associated enhanced conditions of employment, is that it is a mechanism which will also attract and retain high-quality staff.

Under pay-by-performance there is no automatic progression to the top of the grade: progression is dependent upon points being acquired at a performance appraisal interview. The operation of performance-related pay schemes differs widely between employers, but performance-related pay usually works by having an assessed fixed rate for the job, based on precise job evaluation. The pay scale is then built around that fixed rate so that if, for example, the job is 100% then the pay scale can stretch from 90%–110% of that figure. Progression through the range depends on performance determined by performance evaluation. The benefit of this scheme is that, through the identification of key areas, the staff involved will concentrate their attention and performance on the achievement of those key areas. Not all pay increments are consolidated into the basic pay: in some schemes the employee reverts to a set level, and increments to that level are 'earned' each year. In practice, only the outstanding performer will ever reach the top of the range and an unsatisfactory performer will not be able to progress beyond the minimum grade at all.

Performance standards

Performance standards need to be developed for each job so that employees can be made aware of the level of proficiency required. Subjective judgements must be overcome by establishing mutually acceptable standards of performance, such as agreed targets and ways of reaching those targets. The introduction of performance standards can be – though not always – linked to the introduction of financial incentives to make them acceptable to the staff. To gain staff commitment to any such scheme you must involve them in setting the performance standards – standards that are imposed and introduced without consultation will fail to be effective and will be met with hostility.

Although the actual forms used will vary from employer to employer, pay-by-performance operates by listing the principal accountability of the member of staff against the key tasks needed to achieve that accountability. Performance standards or indicators then must also be listed against those key tasks. For example, for a personnel officer a key task will be to recruit, retain and develop staff. Performance indicators might include:

- Average length of time taken to fill vacancies
- Percentage of staff turnover
- Annual production of training needs analysis
- Percentage of training needs met during the period.

The analysis of each job in a pay-by-performance scheme produces a clear statement of purpose for each job, its dimensions and the key areas in which the job-holder is expected to achieve results. These key areas lay the foundation for precise performance appraisal.

Some trade unions have expressed reservations in principle about the introduction of performance-related pay, affecting as it does the guaranteed pay scales. There are also a variety of options for pay-by-performance schemes, ranging from pay linked to performance as discussed above, to team bonuses and merit payments systems. Performance-related pay systems have also been used in the UK to effect a change in organizational behaviour. The recent survey conducted by the Institute of Personnel Management mentioned earlier [4], has noted that, despite growing interest in linking all of the annual pay increase to performance, it has been established that pay-by-performance works more effectively when used with policies to manage employee performance, as in a total performance management strategy. In other words, performance-related pay will only work effectively through a truly motivating pay system,and not one which operates by negative incentives or punitive measures.

Other appraisal methods

Another system of performance appraisal is the little-used multi-appraisal system, which provides a strong motivation base for building staff commitment to improving performance. In this system a number of people in the job network consider the person being evaluated. Usually between 5 and 8 assessors are selected, whose opinions are regarded as useful – they include the direct line manager, peers and subordinate staff; these people assess the person anonymously and the assessments are reviewed at interview, together with a self-assessment done by the member of staff. Obviously this is time-consuming but does give a better overall picture of the performance of the individual under review.

Other financial ways of rewarding merit

It is normal practice for a member of staff who assumes extra duties at a higher level to be paid for that extra responsibility in addition to their normal salary, providing those duties are undertaken over a substantial period of time. In local authority libraries in the UK, the period of time before extra payments can be made is 6 weeks; this allows for normal coverage of duties whilst a line manager is on holiday or otherwise away from the workplace.

One-off single cash payments for special work, usually known as merit awards or honoraria, can be recommended for either permanent or temporary staff who have undertaken work of an exceptional nature, or to reward a particular piece of work rather than all-round performance. These small lump-sum payments are usually made immediately upon completion of the outstanding work and are not consolidated into the salary. Merit awards and honoraria have a temporary beneficial effect upon morale and do encourage staff to respond to exceptional demands made upon them on subsequent occasions.

Paying for such financial incentives is not always easy. Even services and sections that are fee-earning may not have the potential to meet the cost of any pay incentive. Any reward package has therefore to be carefully worked out and included in the salary and wages budget. There is further discussion of other methods of financial reward in *Appraisal related pay* [8], one of the advisory booklets issued by ACAS.

Lamplighters Awards for Excellence

One excellent way of formally managing financial rewards is organized by the Queens Borough Public Library in the USA. The Lamplighters

Awards for Excellence [9] programme is used to acknowledge staff for their commitment to the library via measurable and sustained effort in such things as leadership, teamwork, development of programmes, materials or projects, improvements in public service or operations or significant service to the library. These monetary awards of $1000 are awarded at an annual Service Awards breakfast to an individual who is identified as having made the most outstanding contribution. Library Luminaries awards of $100 are given to employees for meritorious performance – these are people who are also deemed to have made valuable contributions. Nominations to the awards committee can be made by peers, subordinates or supervisors. This scheme has the advantage of involving all staff in the nomination of a financial reward, unlike in the UK, where financial rewards are usually only made on the recommendation of the line manager.

Quality of working life and quality circles

Quality of working life is a method of organizing and managing people. The aim is to gain better staff efficiency and motivation by satisfying staff social and psychological needs; financial rewards, which are only part of the approach, are based on acquired skills and knowledge, rather than job content. This approach involves the active participation of people at all levels through the use of teamwork and increased cooperation; as such, it can greatly enhance the process of communication within the working environment.

Quality circles are usually groups of about eight people who meet together on a regular basis to identify, analyse and solve problems – their objective is to improve the quality of the 'product' to ensure total customer/user satisfaction. Quality circles can contribute greatly to the development of the quality of working life concept by examining work performance and achievements and examining 'quality control'. As stated by Russell and Dale [10], quality circles help to develop staff skills and abilities by creating an environment where everyone is encouraged to fulfil their potential; they also form part of the staff consultative process. Detailed company examples of the contribution that quality circles can make are illustrated by Morland [11].

References

1. Barraclough, Mike and Nilsson, John A. (1991) *Ready drafted employment letters*. Cambridge: Director Books
2. Advisory, Conciliation and Arbitration Service (1988) *Employee appraisal*. London: ACAS
3. American Library Association (1979) *Personnel performance appraisal – a guide for libraries*. Chicago: American Library Association and the Library Administration and Management Association
4. Bevan, Stephen and Thompson, Marc (1991) Performance management at the crossroads. *Personnel Management*, **23**(11), 36–40
5. Industrial Society. *Raising performance* (a video training pack on appraisal interviewing). London: Industrial Society
6. Breakwell, Glynis M. (1990) *Interviewing*. London: British Psychological Society and Routledge
7. Lawson, Ian (1987) *Appraisal and appraisal interviewing*. London: The Industrial Society (Notes for Managers)
8. Advisory, Conciliation and Arbitration Service (1990) *Appraisal related pay*. London: ACAS
9. Queens Borough Public Library (1990) *Leading the way: Lamplighters Awards for Excellence*. New York
10. Russell, Sean and Dale, Barrie (1989) *Quality circles – a broader perspective*. Work Research Unit Occasional Paper No. 43. London: ACAS
11. Morland, Julia (1987) *Quality circles*. London: Industrial Society Press

CHAPTER FOUR

Special employment issues in human resource management

In Chapter 2 we discussed the basic elements of the terms and conditions that must be included in a contract of employment. The American Library Association [1] issues guidelines for professional contracts for the use of institutions that have no formal written agreement, in which all the basic employment terms are specified. This helpful leaflet emphasizes the importance of putting into writing, in the form of a contract, the specific terms of employment of a member of staff. This is good practice, as the kind of contract you issue, whether for full- or part-time, permanent or temporary, for a fixed term or on a casual basis, will affect the employment rights of the member of staff.

Appointing non-permanent staff

There is an increasing use of fixed-term and temporary contracts by employers who do not wish to commit themselves to a permanent increase in their staff numbers but who need someone temporarily to deal with a special project or to cover for a member of staff on long-term sickness or maternity leave. Both sorts of contract can be issued, for example, if you are seeking to introduce a new project and are unsure how successful it may be – if it is not successful you may not wish to have committed yourself, your organization and the library to a permanent and therefore expensive addition to the staff. Thus you should have specific reasons for creating any kind of temporary contract: they should not be used as a method of assessing people who should really be on probation in a permanent post, and temporary employment should be a genuine requirement of the job.

The use of temporary or fixed-term contract staff allows you to retain a degree of flexibility with staffing, although in any real financial consideration you must allow for adaptation time, training time and training costs. Temporary contracts can also keep employees' performance up to standard if they are keen to win an extension or a further contract. You need to be aware that they can also have the reverse effect, where the employee loses interest if it become clear that their contract is not about to be renewed. In these days of high unemployment in the library and information field, it is unlikely that you will have difficulty in attracting suitably qualified and experienced candidates for temporary posts.

Temporary contracts

Temporary contracts are basically very similar to permanent contracts; the basic terms and conditions of employment are often the same as for permanent staff contracts and it is usual for a contractual period of agreed notice to be given should either party need to terminate the employment. For example, staff on temporary contract are subject to the normal probation procedures and, if found not capable or suitable for the post, can be dismissed under these procedures. However, provision may differ, for example, in terms of access to the corporate pension scheme, staff benefits or training provision, other than essential training to do the job for which they are employed. The major difference between permanent and temporary contracts is the rights staff may or may not have on termination of that contract. In issuing any type of temporary contract you should ensure that the contract makes clear – and that the employee understands:

- That the post is temporary
- The expected duration of the post – you do not need to give a precise termination date
- The circumstances that will terminate the appointment, such as the completion of the project or the return from sick leave of the permanent member of staff.

Even when terminating a temporary post, you must be clear about the reason for termination and consider alternative employment for the temporary member of staff, if this is possible and appropriate. It is good practice to discuss this with the member of staff some time before the end of the contract: they have to make arrangements to look for more work and you must ensure that they know what the position is, ideally prior to the notice period. Offering suitable alternative employment before the end of a temporary contract is an important part of the termination procedure, especially if the temporary employee has earned an entitlement to redundancy pay; turning down suitable alternative employment will have an effect on whether they can claim redundancy payments from your organization.

Fixed-term contracts

A fixed-term contract is a contract where the termination date is agreed in advance without either the employer or the employee having to give a period of notice. The date of expiry must be clearly set out in the contract of appointment and the offer accepted in writing; on termination of a fixed-term contract the employee has the right to a written statement outlining why the contract is not being renewed. This appears to be deceptively simple to the uninitiated, but under statutory employment law a fixed-term contract that expires without a renewal is in fact a dismissal, which can allow the member of staff to claim for unfair dismissal and redundancy payments.

However, in the UK, even if a member of staff has a series of fixed-term or temporary contracts, continuity of service to obtain employment protection is established after a 2-year period; continuity of service with one employer is not broken by the issue of a series of different contracts. It is important to remember that 2 years' full-time continuous service for temporary or fixed-term contract staff means the acquisition of statutory rights to redundancy pay, maternity pay, written reasons for dismissal and the right to claim unfair dismissal.

To overcome this problem of the employee accumulating employment rights, you can insert a waiver clause in a contract which is due to last for a year or more, which will have the effect of stopping a member of staff from being able to claim unfair dismissal or redundancy when that contract expires. A waiver clause is so called because it requires the employee to 'waive' their rights to such claims. The provisions of waiver clauses only apply to the date the contract is due to end, and would not apply if you had to terminate the contract earlier than the agreed time for any reason. Because of this you should also include a provision to allow you to terminate the contract, without penalty, before the agreed date: otherwise you will find the member of staff has the right to claim. Staff on fixed-term contracts have a right to receive the normal period of notice of any early termination of their contract.

It is vital to be aware of possible amendments in the employment laws of any country in which you work. As Carr and Kay point out (in *Employment law*) [2], employment legislation is ever-changing and it is not always easy to keep up to date; in the UK, both national and EC case law, for example, can affect employment issues. For this reason, if you are unsure about proper legal procedures or the potential implications of case law, you should always seek guidance from the professional associations or organizations concerned with human resource management, on the current legislative position; such advice can also be obtained from government agencies or their publications, concerned with employment practices.

Appointing casual staff

Casual staff are usually hired for temporary work which occurs in an irregular or unpredictable way, and are generally paid by the hour, only for the work they actually perform. They accrue no holiday or sick leave entitlement and are usually not in post long enough to earn any employment protection. However, depending on the circumstances, there can be disadvantages in using casual staff who may have little or no commitment to the job: a hidden cost of their employment can be the amount of time spent training them. The term 'casual staff' is in current use in the UK public sector – in the LIS private sector such staff would normally be employed as temporary staff and hired from employment agencies.

Differing ways of using working hours

LIS managers should explore flexible ways of using and deploying their staff resources; ultimately this has advantages from the point of view both of recruitment and retention of staff, and service to the customer. Productivity and working time are closely linked and different ways of working can actually improve the service while helping to reduce staffing costs.

It is perfectly in order for an organization to operate more than one working pattern – some organizations are dealing with demographic changes by offering flexitime, or flexible hours, where possible, or by creating zero-hour contracts for staff who are prepared to work on standby arrangements and who can specify their own hours, thus creating banks of trained temporary and casual staff. Others are looking at term-time only working, for staff employed on the same conditions as full-time staff but paid on a pro rata basis. Another system of working is known as the compressed week – this means that the normal weekly working hours are compressed into only three or four working days. Flexitime – that is, the working of any number of hours per day within an overall framework of agreed monthly or weekly hours – has to be tightly monitored to ensure that the freedom is not abused: most of these systems have a core time when staff are expected to be on duty and most are controlled by monitored clocking in and out by the staff. Such staff-friendly timetabling practices are a direct result of difficulties in attracting and retaining staff, and have been matched to accommodate non-standard career patterns, career breaks and career re-entry. Further information about different ways of using working hours can be obtained from ACAS *Hours of work* [3].

An annual hours system of work is used in industry and at least one local authority, Strathkelvin District Council [4], has introduced such a system into the leisure department for operation in the leisure centres. Annual hours is a system under which staff are contracted to work a number of hours per year instead of per week – you do not need to distinguish between holidays and rest days since all the time outside the contracted hours is time off. For example, in any one year, calculating 5 weeks as a holiday period, 1786 hours equates to a 38-hour working week. The annual salary, divided into 12 monthly payments, is made in the normal way, regardless of the number of hours a member of staff may have worked in any one pay period. To enable this system to work properly you need to be able to predict reasonably well the volume and rate of the annual work flow, and to timetable staff to work more and longer shifts at busy times and fewer and shorter shifts when the work flow decreases. This system leads to the more effective use of staffing hours and reduces the demand for temporary staff or overtime payments to cover busy peak periods.

For this reason the introduction of such a system can be unpopular with the staff, since it represents a break with the traditional working week, and a direct effect on staff who are used to receiving overtime payments is a loss of income. The introduction of annual hours needs careful staff consultation, since contracts would need to be renegotiated; any overtime entitlement would most probably need to be bought out – that is, staff paid an agreed lump sum as compensation for potential loss of earnings. The implementation and operation of the scheme must be tightly monitored and reviewed in relation to staff recruitment and retention, working practices and service provision; care must be taken that no-one is timetabled to work longer hours than would be regarded as safe.

Job sharing

The demand for job-sharing opportunities originated in the 1970s, when women who wanted to return to work were prevented from doing so by either domestic responsibilities or the inability to find a part-time post at a level appropriate to their skills and education. Originally introduced to respond to womens' needs, it is now a system of working used by both sexes for people who may wish to study or pursue other careers. It can also be a way to help people who might not otherwise find a job, and can be used successfully in allowing for a period of adjustment before retirement. Job sharing has become widely accepted in the UK, USA and Europe; it operates by the sharing of one full-time post by two people, each of whom is jointly responsible for the job, and who receive the full-time pay and benefits of the post pro rata while working under the same terms and conditions as full-time staff.

There is no best way of job sharing or of splitting a post: indeed, it is the flexibility of job sharing that appeals to employers and employees alike. Many systems work by both job sharers jointly working part of one week; some job sharers choose to work every other week or fortnight, although if the gaps away from work are too long, lack of continuity can cause problems. Experience to date has shown that most job sharers are extremely conscientious and motivated; as they are working part-time they have more energy for the job, and the end result in terms of library work is greater productivity. Whatever system is adopted, the job sharers need a period of overlap to brief each other about their respective responsibilities, and also to liaise with their line manager. Because job sharers are so motivated they tend to be excellent at briefing each other, but having two people in one post can sometimes cause problems for the line manager, for whom the process of communications becomes more complex.

There are some disadvantages to the employer in creating a job-share post. Although the actual costs of employing two people in one post are not significantly higher than employing one person, there is an increase in administrative work. There are, for example, two separate contracts to draft, two staff files to maintain, two sets of references to clear and two medical clearances to obtain. There are also extra training costs involved, since two people will need twice the time for training and staff development opportunities; the work involved in such things as staff appraisal and in coaching and counselling for these staff is doubled, and if you have many such posts there will ultimately be implications for the costs of your training budget. If the job-share post is itself a supervisory post, the staff being supervised could find this confusing or could attempt to play one job sharer off against the other.

These disadvantages, though, should not outweigh the advantages of using job sharers in the library. Job sharing allows you to recruit from a wider mix of applicants, and two people will bring a greater variety of skills to a post than one person. There is usually much flexibility in using the working hours of one job-share post: for example, the two people can actually be on duty at the same time at peak work times, and the job will always be partly covered during holidays and illness. In addition, job sharing is a mechanism that can help you reduce staff turnover and loss of existing trained staff, as it enables staff who might otherwise need to resign to remain in post.

The employer who decides to offer the possibility of job sharing must state as much in the advertisement; indeed, many job sharers come as a pair. However, as an employer you must ensure that the final decision about matching job sharers is yours: you must be sure that you wish to employ both sharers and that you are satisfied they will work well together. This makes the selection interview more complex than if interviewing for a single post-holder. Usually both sharers have separate contracts; both contracts must state that they are sharing one post and you must have a contingency plan built in to cover the problem of filling the other part of the post should one job sharer not meet the probation requirements or decide to leave. One way to resolve this is to make the post part-time only, or to request one job sharer to take over the full-time post if you fail to recruit another suitable sharer. New Ways to Work is a London-based organization and a major source of information on job sharing in the UK [5,6]. A key study of job sharing has been published by the Equal Opportunities Commission [7], and The Library Association also provides practical advice and guidance in their Advice to Members series [8].

Voluntary workers in libraries

In the USA the 'Friends of the Library Groups' are a source of potential volunteers, as are local organizations that may have links with the library. In the UK only some libraries have clearly defined policies covering the use of volunteers. Many trade unions oppose the use of volunteers, since unpaid workers are seen as a threat to paid jobs; for this reason, plans to use volunteers should be discussed with the union. Although there will be exceptions, voluntary workers should not normally be involved in work usually done by the paid staff, nor in work of a confidential nature. On the plus side, the use of volunteers should mean that work or projects might be undertaken that would otherwise not be, and can lead to a good public relations image for the library. For the individual volunteer it can provide a means of gaining valuable hands-on experience, which can be particularly useful for people, usually women, seeking to return to work after a career break.

However attractive the idea may seem, you must take a long hard look at any proposal to use volunteers, and measure the true costs to the library. The use of volunteers can never really be regarded as cost-free – there is always a price to pay in terms of staff time spent in recruitment, training and supervision. Whether you have decided you can use volunteers as a positive action programme or whether you are simply reacting to a request from a possible volunteer, will also define how successful the proposal may be. Good planning is essential if you are to avoid pitfalls. If you are creating a work project suitable for volunteers then you must:

- Clearly define the work to be achieved and design a 'job description'
- Assess the number of work hours involved and the timescale of the project
- Decide on the personal skills and experience needed by any volunteers
- Decide who will supervise the volunteer/s
- Decide how you will 'advertise' for volunteers

- Decide whether you will pay fares and expenses for volunteers
- Check that the library insurance covers the use of volunteers.

In any such programme you must go through an interview process, however informally, to ensure that you are selecting the right kind of volunteer. Volunteers should complete application forms so that you have all the basic information needed for an interview. You will have to explore the times when the volunteer will be available for work, as well as their non-availability. Consideration of mental and physical health can be equally important in the use of volunteers and you should not forget to clarify whether they have any 'unspent' convictions that would affect your decision. You may also wish to consider taking up references.

Although the 'job description' will enable you to decide on the responsibilities of the volunteer, they will need to know how their contribution will affect the overall aims and objectives of the library, and what training will be available. You must also find out what sort of work the volunteeer is not prepared to do. It is really important to explore their reasons for wishing to do voluntary work, and their expectations of the job: if you are unable to meet those expectations it is important to say so at an early stage. Reliability and punctuality on their part are key factors that you will need to establish; however effusive they are at interview, some volunteers can quickly become disillusioned once they start work. This is one of the reasons why you should consider limiting the work – never rely totally on voluntary workers to perform essential work which directly affects the library service: they may become resentful at performing the same work that other people are paid to do. Unlike paid staff, apart from dismissal, you have no ultimate power to discipline them when they fail to turn up for duty or if they are unreliable. Volunteers still need to be evaluated and their worked checked, and you must consider how to terminate the services of an unsatisfactory volunteer and be clear about this policy at the selection interview.

Voluntary workers do need a letter from the library which clearly outlines their duties and the hours they will be expected to work – a kind of contract, albeit unenforceable. Such a letter creates a business like atmosphere and helps to formalize the position of the volunteer; you can also list the conditions under which the voluntary attachment will terminate.

Briefing of the existing staff is essential. The paid staff need to know about the volunteer's work and how the volunteer will fit into the team: they need to know what they can and cannot ask the voluntary worker to do. You should keep accurate statistics about the use of volunteers, the number of people and the hours worked by them, and if they are working on a special project you must make it clear that this work has been achieved with the use of voluntary workers. Too-frequent use of such voluntary workers may also ultimately affect the staffing budget, and the use of untrained volunteers can sometimes serve to devalue the professional work of the library staff. Finally, volunteers need just as much positive thanking for their work as anyone else on the staff, and can be rewarded by such things as staff privileges on book loans and general use of staff facilities.

Employing ex-offenders

Under UK law, ex-offenders must notify any convictions which are regarded as current, to prospective employers. Thus many offenders who have served their sentence and settled their debt to society find it extremely difficult to fit back into normal working life. The Rehabilitation of Offenders Act 1974 allows that after a period of years without reconviction, a person can be considered rehabilitated and the sentence 'spent'. In practice this means the offender is no longer required by law to disclose their conviction to employers except in certain circumstances. The maximum rehabilitation period is 10 years for sentences of between 6 months and $2\frac{1}{2}$ years; lesser sentences merit shorter rehabilitation periods. However, sentences of longer than $2\frac{1}{2}$ years can never be regarded as 'spent', and always have to be declared to the prospective employer.

The Rehabilitation of Offenders Act 1974 (Exception) (Amendments Order) 1986 has extended the range of posts for which an employer can require applicants who will be required to deal with people under the age of 18 years, to reveal details of any criminal convictions, including those which for other purposes would be considered 'spent'. In effect this means that you can apply this order to all applicants for library posts that involve work with children and young people – and some libraries require all staff who have contact with the public to disclose 'spent' convictions. This is wise, since it is easy to overlook this question when arranging internal transfers and promotions, or simply when organizing staff for relief work in another section.

Your general application form may already state that all candidates shortlisted for interview will be required to answer questions as to whether or not they have any unspent previous convictions or criminal charges. A more precise way of dealing with this question, if the post is one for which the applicant must declare 'spent' convictions, is to have a special form which must be signed by a prospective employee to the effect that they either have or have not been convicted of a criminal offence, or been the subject of a conditional discharge, probation order or provisional order. The form should state that any false information or misleading information will disqualify from appointment or, if already appointed, render people liable to dismissal without notice. If they answer in the affirmative then details of the conviction must be supplied, in confidence; you must then make a value judgement about whether or not to employ that person, depending on the nature of the conviction: simply having a previous conviction which has to be declared should not necessarily bar a person from a job. From the point of view of an ex-offender, declaring a previous conviction is not an easy thing to do; they know from experience that knowledge of the conviction can cloud the judgements being made at a selection interview. However, it is far better for an employer to know about previous convictions at this stage than to find out accidentally later. No employee should be allowed to start work without signing such an undertaking. It should go without saying that all information must be regarded as strictly confidential and considered only in relation to the application. If you require more specific information about the workings of this legislation you should refer to the *Guide to the Rehabilitation of Offenders Act* [9].

Staff moves and exchanges

Contracts for large companies or organizations may not identify a single location as a place of work, but rather require the employee to work at any number of unnamed locations within that organization. This allows you to transfer staff from one library to another, according to need. In addition, staff appraisals may have highlighted the need for work experience in other sections: hopefully you will have established a positive and constructive attitude to such transfers. If the move is only for a temporary period you will have to decide how to cover for that person while they are away, or whether you need to effect a joint staff transfer between the two sections. Staff exchanges between sections can be extremely beneficial in improving the understanding of how sections work; in terms of the 'internal customer' approach, there can be long-term benefits for the sections involved. You may also need to move a member of staff either for a second assessment while on probation, or for disciplinary or welfare reasons. In considering staff transfer you must:

- Secure the agreement of the individual by outlining the reasons for the move, the benefits and objectives, the duration and the timescale; also clarify whether any additional expenses incurred by the move will be paid.
- Secure the commitment and support of the line managers involved in any such staff move; this involves the manager who is losing an employee in timetabling adjustments, and additional work for the manager who becomes responsible for the induction, operational training and supervision of the transferred employee.
- Ensure that the line managers fully brief the other members of their teams about the purpose and duration of any staff moves or exchanges.
- Ensure that benefits of any such staff move or exchange are monitored and evaluated with the line managers.This can also be achieved by debriefing sessions with the staff involved, and the results used in planning any further moves and exchanges.

When the work of the library or information unit interlinks with the demands or needs of another organization, there may be valid operational reasons to organize staff training attachments to that organization. In this case you will need a written cooperation contract agreeing the objectives, timing and duration of these joint staff exchanges which, as always, will need to be carefully monitored and evaluated.

Staff exchanges at international level are very much more complex to organize. Such exchanges are rarely initiated by employers: usually the impetus comes from the employee. There are always benefits to be gained from this sort of exchange, notably in the arrival of new ideas and methods of work and a reinvigorated and enthusiastic member of staff, but the complexities of such exchanges must be carefully investigated by both the library and the member of staff involved prior to any agreement being reached. As an employer you must be sure of the expected benefits and improvement in your member of staff and that your service will not suffer while that person is away. If you are receiving another national as part of the temporary exchange, you must ensure you have the time to organize a thorough in-service training programme. Such exchanges can involve you in a great deal of work and planning; you may need to obtain a permit from the Department of Employment and you may find yourself organizing such things as accommodation, hospitality and educational library visits outside your own organization. This does not mean that you should be put off organizing international exchanges, but you must be aware of the extra effort needed. Requests for such exchanges are usually advertised in the professional press and further information can be obtained from professional LIS associations.

Work permits and extensions to stay

When employing a new member of staff it is your responsibility to ensure that they are entitled to work in the UK. You may safely accept applications from nationals of the European Community, since they have the right to work anywhere within the other member states. Any commonwealth national between the ages of 17 and 27 years can apply for a working holiday in the UK for up to 2 years, to work full-time for half of that period or part-time for the whole of that period; the actual length of any working holiday status is granted at the discretion of the immigration officer, who has to be assured that the applicant has enough resources to support themselves during their period in the UK. Applicants can apply for a visa prior to arrival in the UK, or can apply at immigration at their port of arrival. Commonwealth applicants who have a grandparent born in the UK and have documentary evidence to prove this, are entitled to work in the UK for up to 4 years, after which they can apply for permanent residence. It is always wise to check the right to work of a foreign national by asking to see the entry stamp on their passport; this will clearly state how long they can remain in the country and whether they have the right to work.

From October 1991 a new Work Permit Scheme operates in the UK. This scheme enables employers to employ people who would otherwise be prevented from working in the UK by the immigration rules. Applications for work permits are now made direct to the Department of Employment, instead of the Home Office, as was previously the case.

The Department issues a guide for employers [10] which is available from the Overseas Labour Section. Work permits are not usually issued for unskilled or semi-skilled jobs, or for jobs which can be reasonably filled by EC nationals. If you do need to obtain a work permit on behalf of a prospective employee, it is essential to ensure that you have a valid reason for employing an overseas national. You will be required to justify your application by stating why you have been unable to fill the post with a UK or EC national; in the case of an application to renew a permit you will need to explain why you have been unable to train or transfer an existing member of staff – this includes providing evidence of unsuccessful recruitment advertising. Applications for permits or renewals for more than 4 years are very carefully vetted since, as we have seen above, this is the length of time needed to obtain settlement rights in the UK.

Work permit applications which are not subject to undue delays include transfers within international companies, such as career development posts, board-level posts, posts involving inward investment posts where the occupation is recognized as being in short supply. In a period of high unemployment it is unlikely that most library and information science posts could not be filled from within the existing workforce.

If you are offering UK training or work experience to an overseas national other than an EC national, then your application should be for a permit under the separate Training and Work Experience Scheme [11] details of which can be obtained from the Overseas Labour Section of the Employment Department. Apart from EC member states, whose nationals are able to take up posts in any other member state, LIS managers operating in other countries should check with the appropriate government department if they wish to obtain a work permit for an overseas national.

Maternity rights

Working women who become pregnant are entitled to various rights and privileges under UK law. Employees must be given reasonable paid time off for antenatal care, subject to a medical appointment and if requested, the production of a certificate confirming the pregnancy. This facility must be granted to all women regardless of their length of service or hours of work. Failure to allow a woman such paid time off means that she can take a complaint to an industrial tribunal within 3 months of the date of the medical appointment.

The maternity provision set out in the Employment Protection (Consolidation) Act 1978, include the unfair dismissal provisions relating to maternity leave, which are discussed in the next chapter. A woman at work is also entitled to receive statutory maternity pay, which is payable under the Social Security Act 1986 [12]. Amended regulations are issued from time to time by HMSO, and updating regulations relating to statutory maternity pay benefits are published annually. To be sure of obtaining up to date information about any amendments and rates of pay, you should contact the local office of the Department of Social Security. This is particularly pertinent when considering the EC Directive on maternity provisions, which at the time of writing, had not yet been adopted by the UK.

In the UK, statutory maternity pay can be claimed by women who have been continuously employed for at least 26 weeks before the expected week of confinement, and who are still in employment in what is known as the qualifying week – that is, the 15th week before the baby is due. A woman must have stopped work in order to obtain the payments, which you are obliged to pay even if she has stated that she does not intend to return to work after the birth. Since you are acting on behalf of the Department of Social Security in making these payments, any statutory maternity payments made by you can be recovered.

Both full-time and part-time employees are entitled to claim the 18 weeks statutory maternity pay, which can be paid at two rates. The lower rate, which is reviewed by the government every year, is paid when the employee has fulfilled the 26 weeks' continuous employment requirement but has not completed 2 years' service for full-time employees or 5 years for part-time employees. Women who have worked full time – that is at least 16 hours per week – for the same employer for a continuous period of 2 years, or women who have worked part time – between 8 and 16 hours a week – for at least 5 years, may be entitled to the higher rate for the first 6 weeks; this is 90% of the weekly earnings. Statutory maternity pay is subject to the normal deductions for tax and national insurance contributions.

Some employers also have occupational maternity schemes which can run parallel with the statutory maternity scheme and which offer pregnant women improved terms and conditions. Depending on the benefits offered by the occupational scheme, the regulations can stipulate that a woman must remain in post for a specified period of time after her return from maternity leave, otherwise the occupational scheme payments may have to be refunded.

The rights given to women under current UK legislation include the right to return to work, provided she has worked for the same employer for at least 2 years before the beginning of the 11th week before the birth. Some occupational schemes give this right after only 1 year's service. Subject to certain conditions, women retain the right to return to their job at any time within 29 weeks following the birth.

As a UK employer, if the woman has complied with all the conditions required of her, then you must allow her to return to her job. Failure to allow her to do this will effectively mean that you are dismissing her. If her actual job is no longer available because of redundancy, then you must offer her suitable alternative work – that is, suitable and appropriate for the woman and under the same terms and conditions as her previous job – otherwise she will be able to claim unfair dismissal. However, if she rejects such alternative employment, she can lose her right to redundancy payments. If a woman accepts redundancy during maternity leave this ends the employer's contractual obligations to both occupational maternity pay and her right to return to work; the payment of statutory maternity pay is not affected and may continue to the end of the maternity pay period.

It is at about this time that many women begin to seriously consider returning to work part time or as a job sharer. In fact, they have no automatic right to return to work under different conditions, such as reduced hours, but you must give careful consideration to any such request; the advantages of retaining a trained and motivated employee are numerous and should not be overlooked, but case law now means that refusal to consider such requests may be considered as sex discrimination. This should not stop you refusing such a request as long as you can justify that your decision was reasonable and did not unjustly discriminate against the woman. Would your decision have been the same, for example, if the request had come from a male employee?

From the point of view of work planning, the earlier you know about a woman's proposed absence because of maternity leave the better. However, a woman need only give 21 days' notice of the date she intends to stop work, to claim her right of return. You may not be able to reorganize the work or hire temporary staff in such a short period, so it is useful to have established good general communications with staff so that you get to know such information in plenty of time to replan the work effectively.

In recruiting a temporary replacement to cover maternity leave you must make it absolutely clear, at interview and in writing, that the employment will be terminated on the return to work of the absent employee. Most advertisements for this kind of temporary post state quite clearly that the post is to cover a temporary maternity leave vacancy. If, at a later stage, the woman on maternity leave does not actually return to work and you do not wish to retain the temporary employee, you should readvertise the post as a permanent vacancy. This procedure enables the temporary employee to apply for the permanent post in open competition with any other applicants. Should you ultimately decide to appoint another person, be sure that you are able to justify this decision as fair and reasonable.

The European Community Social Chapter stipulates 14 weeks' maternity leave, with the right to return to work, for all pregnant employees regardless of length of service. It also stipulates no dismissal on the grounds of pregnancy and the maintenance of all employment rights and benefits while on maternity leave. It should be noted that although the UK had voted not to adopt the Social Chapter, nevertheless maternity provisions in the UK will be affected by the new EC Directive on maternity provisions. Within the EC some countries handle maternity rights very generously. For example, in The Hague [13] breastfeeding women are allowed up to a quarter of their working week to feed their child, which can either be done at home or in a special room at work. General parental caring rights, in addition to maternity rights, extend to 50% time off work for between 1 and 6 months while receiving 87% of the normal salary. In addition, the parent of a child under 12 months is entitled to a maximum of 20 days' unpaid leave to care for the child. Such generous parental leave entitlements do encourage employees to remain in post, and have distinct advantages for the employer in retaining trained staff. As an employer you should ensure good working practices by allowing a pregnant woman easier working conditions during her pregnancy; for example, sympathetic consideration should be given to a woman who requests not to work long hours in front of a visual display unit, if this causes her stress and worry about the health of her unborn child.

References

1. Jennerich, Elaine Z. *Guidelines for professional contracts.* Chicago: American Library Association
2. Carr, C. J. and Kay, P. (1990) *Employment law* 5th edn. London: Pitman
3. Advisory, Conciliation and Arbitration Service (1989) *Hours of work.* London: ACAS
4. Pickard, Jane (1991) Annual hours: a year of living dangerously? *Personnel Management*, **23**(8), 38–43
5. *Job sharing: a guide for employers.* (1983) London: New Ways to Work
6. *Job sharing: putting policies into practice – the local authority experience.* (1987) London: New Ways to Work
7. Equal Opportunities Commission (1981) *Job-sharing: improving the quality and availability of part-time work.* Manchester: EOC
8. Library Association *Job sharing: advice to members.* London: Library Association
9. *Guide to the Rehabilitation of Offenders Act 1974.* (1991) London: HMSO
10. Department of Employment: Overseas Labour Section (1992) *Immigration Act 1971: guide to employers; work permit applications.* London: HMSO
11. Department of Employment (1989) *Guide for employers (training and work experience scheme: employment of overseas nationals in the United Kingdom).* London: HMSO
12. Department of Social Security (1987) *Guide to maternity benefits.* London: HMSO
13. Gemeente Den Haag (1991) *Kort & Bondig.* The Hague:

CHAPTER FIVE

Termination, redundancy and dismissal of staff

You should make sure that employees are aware of their obligations when they wish to terminate their employment. If a member of staff is leaving voluntarily, they should submit a letter of resignation giving you the correct period of notice according to their contract. Some people object to giving reasons for leaving in this letter: although this is not strictly necessary it can be important from the organizational point of view if the cause of resignation is for better opportunities or improved conditions of work, since this will alert you to market factors which will ultimately affect your organization's ability to recruit and retain suitable staff. In addition, the employee should be made aware that the letter of resignation is retained on their personal file: prospective future employers may ask very specific questions about why an employee left their employment, and if this is not recorded the referee will be unable to answer, and this could be to the detriment of the employee. You may also need to keep such information for statistical purposes – if your staff turnover rate is high it can signal any number of problems, from poor selection procedures to the operation of ineffectual line management skills. If staff are resigning for better pay and prospects elsewhere, then you need this information to justify improvements to pay and conditions to keep up to date with the employment market.

Requests to leave without working a period of notice

Once an employee finds a new post their interest and concerns veer toward that new post and their commitment to the existing job diminishes; the new employer may be anxious for them to start work quickly, and the employee may ask if they can leave without working through the period of notice.

You must evaluate the staffing situation for yourself. Both employees and employers can waive their rights of notice and there will be occasions when you can let people go. There will be times when an employee is leaving for reasons of career development or because of a change in personal circumstances, and on such occasions it is good practice to allow them to leave feeling well disposed towards your organization. However, the period of notice is there to give you time to recruit a new member of staff; many notice periods are barely adequate to do this. If you really are unable to manage with your remaining staff resources, you are within your rights to insist that the person work out their full period of notice. So that you retain the employee's goodwill you should carefully explain the reasons for your refusal. Failure of a member of staff to work out a period of notice as agreed in their contract of employment can leave you with few penalties, except in the reference where, if asked, you can state that the person left without giving proper notice – a possible warning sign to any future employer.

Procedures when a member of staff resigns

The resignation of a member of staff involves you in a certain amount of administration. Apart from advising the personnel department, if you have one, this will include:

- Checking on final salary payments, including any overtime, enhanced payments or expenses due, and preparing tax documents
- Checking on any outstanding holiday that has either to be taken before the resignation date or paid for by your organization
- Notifying the pension section, if this is relevant, and cancelling other benefits that the employee is receiving, such as medical and health insurance, car allowances, etc.
- Collecting and cancelling identity passes; collecting keys
- The writing of references for the individual
- Arranging an exit interview to re-evaluate the job and revise the job description/alter working practices
- Advertising the vacancy/arranging for temporary replacement

- Checking on forwarding address, notifying staff newsletter of resignation and closing personnel files
- Drafting a final letter to the member of staff to thank them for their work while in your employment.

Writing a reference

References are usually requested from line managers when staff or former staff apply for new posts and are being called to a selection interview; very often the date of the interview is provided, accompanied by a request for the reference to reach the writer before the interview takes place. The reference is used as part of the selection process and for this reason you should respond to such requests as a matter of urgency. If, for any reason, you are unable to meet the requested deadline, a quick telephone call to the writer should be sufficient for an initial verbal reference. If the candidate is successful, a full written reference can always be provided at a later date.

References essentially have to be honest and factual and provide some degree of assessment about the candidate's future potential. They should not give falsely favourable information but neither should they make derogatory statements; preferred practice is to either give a positive reference or to refuse to give a reference at all, apart from a pure statement of fact about employment dates and posts held – indeed it is the policy of some organizations to refuse to provide a reference rather than provide a bad one. More often than not, providing a reference full of criticisms of a former employee will reflect adversely on the writer, rather than on the employee. In requesting a reference the organization will normally state if it is the policy to allow the staff access to information provided by referees, or whether the information is requested in confidence; custom and practice seems to be in favour of allowing staff full access to the contents of their files.

In drafting a reference you may reasonably divide the letter into separate sections:

- The first paragraph, which is used to identify the nature of the letter and the person about whom you are writing.
- The second paragraph, in which you should state how long you have known the candidate and in what capacity, and give details of their current work. In some difficult cases you may choose to end the

reference at this stage if you only wish to provide necessary factual information. However, it is more useful if you can state here any exceptional work, tasks or projects the candidate has undertaken, or specific personal skills they possess.

- The third paragraph should relate the candidate's work, experience, skills/attributes to the new job description, if supplied. Some potential employers will ask specific questions about the candidate's experience and capabilities which you should endeavour to answer from your knowledge of the person. Rather than reply in a negative fashion, you may prefer to make no comment.
- Other prospective employers will ask specific questions about sick leave or absences, punctuality or standards of behaviour. Your answers here will most certainly affect whether the candidate will be successful or not; you may temper your remarks by adding more details: 'Miss B. has had 21 days' sick leave in the last 12 months due to hospitalization. The problem has now been resolved and she has had no further time off'. Such an approach is more helpful than simply reporting that fact that the employee had 21 days' sick leave in the period under review.
- The final paragraph can be used to state your own opinion and endorsement of the candidate for the job in question.

There is a difference between supplying a reference to a future employer and supplying an educational reference. Such references are used to help assess suitability and ability to follow a particular course or vocational qualification. You do not need to supply details of existing qualifications held by the applicant, which will already be known, but instead concentrate on the person's individual qualities of perseverance, ability to cope under stress, desire to complete the course and general motivation, that have led them to apply for the course.

Exit interviews

Sometimes referred to as termination interviews, these are extremely useful management tools. They provide a chance to assess with an outgoing post-holder whether the balance of the work content needs to be reviewed or altered; they are important indicators in establishing reasons for high staff turnover. The format of the interview can centre around the job, opportunities for training and development and possible improvements to work practices; this in turn leads to an updating of the job description, which will be necessary before the post is advertised. There are almost always two reasons for an employee's leaving their job – the stated reason and the undeclared reason [1]. Identifying any underlying reasons for a resignation can be difficult, but carefully phrased questions about the job content may help to elucidate problems of management style and job organization that warrant further investigation. Many people will not wish to criticize their line manager, but in talking about their job any difficulties or problems will emerge in their own right. A personal exit interview is a more successful method of elucidating information about a job than using a questionnaire or requiring the completion of a form – such methods do not allow you easily to seek clarification on specific points raised, nor to identify any potential employee bias. Quite apart from these matters, the exit interview gives you a chance to formally thank the member of staff for their service.

Handling normal staff retirement

Your overall personnel planning policy will have alerted you well in advance of any staff retirement due to take place at normal retirement age. Administration for matters such as pension payments or notification to the tax authorities need to be sorted out well in advance. As part of the process of retirement you should help the person to prepare for change. As discussed earlier, preparation for retirement can be facilitated by phased retirement using job sharing or part-time work. Short courses which look at the positive aspects of retirement are now available to help people adjust and plan for retirement; these are generally better if attended well in advance of the actual retirement date. Such courses explore the opportunities that retirement can bring as well as examining personal financial management, health issues and developing interests and social contacts. There are also many publications available that give practical advice on all of these issues, for example Ream's *Enjoying retirement* [2]. An exit interview is essential, as for all staff, to consider redesigning the job before it is advertised, but also staff who are retiring need to be told that their service has been of value.

Facing up to redundancy

Unfortunately, redundancy, also known as 'downsizing' or 'letting people go' is now a frequent occurrence. Making staff redundant is one of the most difficult tasks for a manager to face; possible redundancies cause actual disruptions to the work flow and the trauma and upheaval remain long after the redundant staff have gone. How you handle potential and actual redundancies will have an important effect on the morale, motivation and performance of the remaining workforce.

Reasons for redundancy

Most reasons for redundancy occur when either the employer ceases to carry out the work for which the person was employed, or the need for the work has ceased or diminished; the latter situation can occur when organizational restructuring takes place and substantially alters the duties and responsibilities of a job. If a job remains basically unaltered, a member of staff would normally be expected to accept the revised duties under their existing contract; if a job has greatly changed this may mean that it is unreasonable to ask staff to carry on, or that new or different skills are needed, in which case the member of staff would be declared redundant. Proper human resource planning may help to alleviate the need for compulsory redundancies by such things as retraining, redeployment, restrictions on further recruitment and calls for voluntary redundancy or early retirement; the existence of an agreed redundancy procedure which covers such matters will help to ensure that employees are treated fairly. In a period of uncertainty and upheaval, requests for early retirement or volunteers for redundancy need careful handling and forethought: you should consider putting restrictions on applications, otherwise more people may apply than you wish to release; nor do you want to run the risk of losing people whose skills and experience are necessary for the continued efficient operation of the service.

Employers are increasingly turning to outplacement agencies to help resolve re-employment problems for those made redundant; such agencies offer practical help and guidance to staff who are facing redundancy or who have been made redundant; depending on the level of the staff this may involve a range of support activities from assistance with the drafting of a curriculum vitae, personal profiling, identifying skills and aptitudes, circulating details to prospective employers, practical help with applications and job interviews, or major career development programmes. Because of the recent growth in such agencies and the consequent demands being made upon them a code of conduct has been developed by the Institute of Personnel Management [3] to ensure a high standard of professional responsibility and behaviour by those operating such services.

In compulsory redundancy situations staff need to understand how the selection procedures for redundancy operate; the concept of 'last in, first out' is usually readily understood and accepted, although if used indiscriminately you may end up losing staff whose skills are needed and retaining staff who do not have the right abilities for future development. Other criteria can be aptitude for the work, performance standards, attendance or disciplinary records. Establishing an internal appeals procedure will enable employees who feel they have been unfairly selected for redundancy to seek solution to the problem without referring their complaint to an industrial tribunal.

The responsibilities of employers in handling redundancies are clearly set out in the employment protection legislation, and are quite distinct from the employer's responsibility to make redundancy payments. In the UK, the employer is required to consult with any recognized trade union about prospective redundancies even if the staff concerned are not members of that union and the staff are volunteering for redundancy; this may not necessarily be the same in other countries. However, even though the UK legislation refers specifically to consultation with the trade union, it is good practice to have a thorough consultation process, which should take place at the earliest oportunity with both the trade unions and with the individuals concerned. Recent tribunal case results in the UK would indicate that there is an obligation to consult with individuals.

Under UK law you will be expected to notify the trade union, in writing, of the reasons for the redundancies, the number and description of employees affected, and the total number of employees of any such description employed. They also have the right to know the timetable and the proposed method of selecting staff and carrying out the redundancies. There are agreed minimum periods of consultation: 30 days are required for consultation if between 10 and 99 staff are to be made redundant in one establishment over a period of 30 days or less. Longer periods are laid down if larger numbers of staff are involved, but there is no laid-down consultation period if fewer than 10 staff are to be made redundant. The trade union may wish to raise points about the redundancies in order to lessen the effect they will have on the remaining staff and their workloads; they will also wish to to ensure that the redundancies are handled fairly. In any event, you should certainly have gone through a consultation process before writing to employees to give them formal notice of redundancy.

Consultation with the staff is of the utmost importance. You may be encountering redundancy situations for the first time and you must learn how to counsel individuals effectively and sensitively. Pauline Crofts [4] reports that most professionals concerned with outplacement agree that it is the line manager that should deliver the news of redundancy to the staff. At either group meetings or individual interviews you must decide:

• How to set the right climate for the interview/meeting
• How you will open and close the interview/meeting
• How to handle potential aggression. The uncertainty of the situation upsets the staff; many will want to let off steam, although the anger will not necessarily be aimed at you personally. In such situations you must simply allow time for staff to work out their anger/ resentment. Acceptance of the redundancy situation becomes easier once accurate information is available about personal circumstances and termination dates, although commitment at work and productivity at this time will inevitably diminish.

You will need to outline the proposed action programme and procedures leading up to the redundancies and describe any facilities you can offer staff to help them find alternative employment.

If large numbers of staff are involved and no personnel professional is on hand to assist, you should arrange to see each person individually and provide each one with a package of information, including:

• A provisional calculation of their redundancy entitlements. In the UK this is based on the number of complete years of service, the weekly rate of pay and the age of the person. For example, for each completed year of service staff may be entitled to:
   $\frac{1}{2}$ week's pay for each year between 18 and 21 years
   1 week's pay for each year between 22 and 40 years
   $1\frac{1}{2}$ week's pay for each year between 41 and 64 years.

Service before the age of 18 years is not eligible for redundancy payments and reductions of one-twelfth for each month after the employee's 64th birthday are made for a person who is within 12 months of normal retirement age. Redundancy pay is not subject to tax.

To qualify for redundancy payment, staff must usually have worked continuously with the same employer for at least 2 years, for 16 hours per week or more, or have completed at least 5 years' service for 8 hours a week or more.

Ex-gratia payments based on the above calculations, or a proportion of the calculation, can be made to staff who do not qualify for the official redundancy payments. The goodwill thus established is important in maintaining and restoring the morale of any remaining staff.

- Any additional payments. These might include payment for outstanding holiday or payment in lieu of notice; the employee who is declared redundant still has the right to a formal period of notice.
- Details about how and when these payments will be made.
- Advice about registering as unemployed; people so registered are credited with national insurance contributions, which ultimately affects their state benefits.
- Their statutory right to reasonable paid time off to look for other work or to attend interviews. A particular problem here is that staff who find another post will lose their rights to redundancy payments if they resign before the redundancy date. You will need to advise employees whether there is any flexible approach to declaring an employee redundant at an earlier date – care needs to be taken in doing this, since staff resources could be depleted while you still have a service to operate.
- Guidance and counselling about finding another post, including your willingness to provide a reference.

In a large organization you may be able to consider redeployment to other posts: you must establish whether staff wish to be redeployed, retrained if appropriate, or to accept redundancy. Suitable employment is deemed to be similar in pay, status, location, environment and hours of work, although you can arrange to have the salary of the person protected if the rate of pay is less than they are earning. You will need to know about vacancies, actual and expected, and to cooperate with other managers to give priority to employees who are facing redundancy. You can also retain staff in a temporary capacity if you know that a suitable vacancy will occur in the near future and the person has skills and experience that will be useful. In terms of the salary budget this can be costly, since the member of staff is supernumerary while in a temporary post, but the financial cost can be offset in terms of human resource management, because of the goodwill felt by the individual concerned and other staff not immediately affected.

Staff who accept a written offer of suitable alternative work have the right to a trial period of 4 weeks in that post, or possibly longer if training is needed, without losing their rights to redundancy payment if they decide the job is unsuitable. This trial period also enables you to assess their suitability for the new post, and you must ensure that they have the necessary skills or potential to carry out its full duties; you can jointly agree to extend this trial period, but the employee loses the right to redundancy payment if they remain in post after the agreed extension date; depending on the circumstances, staff who refuse the offer of suitable alternative employment can also lose their right to redundancy payment. Further constructive information can be obtained from ACAS [5].

Grievance procedures

At some stage of your career you will almost certainly have to deal with a member of staff who has a grievance about their employment; this can include problems with workload, conditions of work or terms of employment, or clashes of personality. Employers are required to bring to the attention of their staff the grievance procedure arrangements operating within their organization: this normally happens as part of the induction process. The grievance procedure is usually written into the staff handbook or manual, where it can be easily consulted, and creates a mechanism by which employees can raise matters in which they feel they are being unfairly or unjustly treated. A grievance procedure lays down the way in which an employee can formally raise their grievance, a timescale by which the employer has to respond, and includes details of an appeal system. The objective should be to resolve the problem as fairly and as quickly as possible, in order to achieve a positive outcome.

In reality, the effective line manager should be aware of interactions between staff and observe abnormal behaviour or attitudes which are an indication of potential unsatisfactory situations and attempt to resolve them; the line manager has a responsibility to sort out such problems before they develop into greater problems and official grievances. It is always better to deal with staff problems as and when they occur; if left, a grievance can escalate and become more difficult to resolve. When dealing with any grievance you must ensure that you do not attempt to prejudge the problem. Take the time to listen to what the employee has to say, and make sure that all the facts, as reported to you, are correct before you reach any decision. Remember there may be another side or perspective to the matter and this will need to be thoroughly investigated before any fair resolution of a grievance is possible. In order to create time for reflection, it is probably better to tell the employee that you will need to investigate the situation. As grievances need to be resolved quickly, you must come back to the employee at an agreed time or date without any undue delays.

Whatever decision you reach it will have to be within organizational policy; you must ensure that everyone involved knows about the outcome and is reasonably satisfied. If a grievance goes beyond this informal stage, the grievance procedure should refer to the employee's right to ask for a hearing at agreed higher levels, the right to be represented by a third party, usually a trade union representative, and the right of appeal at each stage.

Disciplinary codes

Disciplinary codes, which are part of the contract of employment if the organization has more than 20 staff, provide a way of establishing accepted norms of attendance, conduct and performance at work, and agreed fair and consistent methods of dealing with infringements of those standards. The codes also define what actions can be taken if these standards are not met; usually the intention is to be corrective rather than punitive. Even so, in setting down standards it is important to define the degree of seriousness, and to list those offences for which dismissal might be justified at the first proven offence – usually stealing, assault, serious breaches of the safety regulations and fraud for financial gain. Other regulations will cover such things as:

- Timekeeping and absenteeism
- Negligence in behaviour and the performance of duties

- Discrimination against another for reasons of race or sex
- Being under the influence of drink or drugs at work
- Unauthorized use of equipment and materials such as photocopiers, telephones, franking machines, etc.

Since it is impossible to list every possible offence, most codes include a 'catch-all' section which enables disciplinary action to proceed for offences not specifically quoted. It is essential to clearly list the staff to whom the code applies. Explanation of the code and its operation should also be part of the induction training and, as with everything, the code should be reviewed from time to time to make sure it is operating effectively.

All staff are normally subject to an agreed disciplinary code. However, if you are dealing with an alleged breach of the code by a trade union official, in order to avoid the possibility of being seen to attack the union, it would be wiser to consult with another union official before proceeding beyond the oral warning stage.

Counselling concerning possible disciplinary action

If there does appear to be a breach of the disciplinary code, the manager should gather all the facts to consider whether a case for formal disciplinary action exists; when all is considered there may be no case, or the manager may decide to deal with the problem informally. Not all breaches of the disciplinary code are intentional: there might be an underlying problem which is causing a member of staff to behave in an uncharacteristic manner. Most managers initially attempt to deal with a problem by counselling, discussions and informal warnings. The objective of counselling a member of staff should be to help them improve; any criticism should be constructive and care taken that the counselling session does not turn into a disciplinary interview by ensuring that the interview takes place in a non-hostile environment. However, you should keep signed and dated notes of any counselling sessions, together with details of the suggested course of action to remedy the situation; these notes can be used to monitor the progress of the person involved and they are also evidence of your unbiased attempts to seek an early and effective solution. Whatever informal action has taken place, it is unlikely that undocumented procedures will be taken into account at any later stage.

Dealing with staff sickness and absence

The documentation of counselling sessions is particularly necessary if you are dealing with an employee whose health is giving cause for concern but who is trying to hold on to their job. If improvements are required in, say, attendance, this should be made clear to the employee with a statement of the outcome if no improvements are forthcoming. In fairness to the employee you could explore the possibility of reduced hours or part-time work; alternatively you could consider obtaining a medical report about a person's suitability for the work or their prospects for a full recovery – this will help both you and the member of staff reach a satisfactory decision about their future. If it does come to dismissal, your first responsibility rests with your employer and you cannot retain a person who, for whatever reason, is unable to perform their job adequately and is unlikely to be able to do so in the foreseeable future. Sometimes the only way to deal with ill health is via the disciplinary code, although it should be emphasized that you will not be disciplining the person because they are genuinely ill but because they are unable to do the job for which you are paying them. Needless to say, such cases must be treated with the utmost sensitivity and confidentiality.

Disciplinary code procedures

If counselling, for whatever reason, has not been successful you have no alternative but to pursue the disciplinary code. Usually most codes follow a system of 'progressive' discipline – this means that there are several stages in the disciplinary procedures. ACAS [6] recommends at least three formal stages before dismissal: verbal warnings, first written warning and final warning or disciplinary suspension; most of these stages operate within a timeframe stated in the code, thus a verbal warning might be valid for 6 months, a first written warning for 12–18 months, and a final written warning for 36 months. This does not mean that all stages have to be followed every time: depending on the gravity of any proven case you can issue any appropriate level of warning, or indeed dismiss if the offence is serious enough. A similar pattern of disciplinary stages is followed in many other countries, including the USA, although the timescales may vary. A proven re-offence within the period of a live warning may indicate the need to issue the next level of warning automatically; thus a proven re-offence within the period of a final written warning could mean instant dismissal, and you would have a duty to warn members of staff of this implication. However, for periods of good behaviour some of the warning time can be commuted – for example, a period of good behaviour could reduce a written warning after 12 months to the status of a verbal warning; this would have implications should the person re-offend. One common misconception concerns the verbal warning: many people think that these need not be recorded, but in fact a verbal warning is a stage of the disciplinary code and must be recorded in writing, both to the individual and on their file for the duration of its validity.

Whatever the nature of the code, if you have one you must follow all the agreed procedures; if you do not do so, then you risk losing your case, however justifiable, through incorrect application of the code. You must therefore fully understand how to implement your own code and proceed with every action as laid down.

Before proceeding with any disciplinary action you need to:

- Assess the nature of the allegation to decide which part of the disciplinary code has been breached.
- Ascertain that the allegation can be substantiated by checking the facts, taking statements and collecting relevant documentation.
- Instruct the member of staff, in writing, to attend a disciplinary interview and advise them of their right to be represented. This letter must outline the nature of the offence and state which part of the code has been breached. Proper notice of the interview must be given – a minimum is 48 hours – to allow them to prepare their defence. You may wish to send this letter recorded delivery; you can require the person to acknowledge receipt of the letter and that they will be attending on the day and time specified. If the member of staff refuses to cooperate, then you should hold the hearing in their absence, based on the available information, having informed them of your intention to do so.
- Consider whether the offence is serious enough to warrant a suspension from duty pending investigation; this should be in cases where there could be a risk to the safety or security of others.

The aims of the disciplinary interview

The aims of the disciplinary interview are to:

- Discover the truth of the situation
- Listen to the employee's defence
- Establish whether the member of staff is guilty or innocent of the alleged offence
- Ascertain any extenuating circumstances
- Determine what action to take under the disciplinary code, if guilty
- Put that action into practice.

Conducting a disciplinary interview

It should go without saying that the interview must be conducted in a suitable location away from interruptions, and that if you are calling witnesses that they have been notified in writing of the time and place of the hearing; it would be wise to confirm that witnesses are willing and able to attend. As all disciplinary hearings cause some disruption to the flow of work, a useful strategy is to hold the interview towards the end of the working day – this allows a potentially emotional member of staff to go straight home, rather than return to their place of work or to confront other staff who are bound to know what has taken place and who will be curious about the outcome. It is wise to have another person with you at the interview, particularly if the member of staff is to be represented, either to make accurate notes or to act as a witness for you. If you are conducting the interview it is essential that you are well prepared; you must take some time beforehand to study the disciplinary code itself to ensure that you are acting correctly during the interview, to gather all your supporting evidence and papers together, and to rehearse how you will handle the interview. As interviewer you must ensure that you control the interview, that you remain calm and impartial, and that you are prepared to listen and hear what the member of staff has to say; you should ensure that you create a neutral but firm stance.

You should start the interview by:

- Introducing everyone present
- Explaining their role in the interview

- Outlining the reason for the interview, itemizing which part of the code has been breached and the alleged offence
- Explaining the procedures and structure of the interview.

If the allegation is not admitted, time must be allowed for the employee and their representative to put forward their case and for the calling of witnesses. If the interview becomes emotionally charged it is sometimes better to adjourn temporarily before starting again, but no amount of putting off will get away from the fact that you must reconvene the hearing eventually.

Having listened to all the evidence you should:

- Sum up the various points that have been made concerning the offence
- Review issues raised by the employee
- Review any matters that may need to be checked.

You will need to adjourn the proceedings to allow you to come to a decision: if the facts are in dispute you must weigh up the balance of the evidence to establish which version is accurate. If you decide a member of staff is guilty, your next course of action must be to determine the appropriate level of penalty, according to the seriousness of the situation. If you find the member of staff is not guilty, you must advise them of this and remove all reference to the matter from the files.

In finding someone guilty of an offence it is important that you are seen to be consistent in applying the code and its penalties, and that the penalty is reasonable according to the circumstances. You must then advise the employee of the outcome of the disciplinary hearing and of their right to appeal – you do this at the end of the interview and conform the decision in writing, outlining which section of the code has been breached, the status of the action and how long it will remain in force. The action may include demotion, a suspension from the post or a disciplinary transfer. It is important to warn the member of staff of the outcome if their standard of performance and behaviour does not improve: to this end you may wish to set up some training if appropriate, and to consider monitoring the position.

You must arrange to set up an active policy to tag all disciplinary letters on personal files and to remove them once the penalty time has expired: forward entries in diaries is a good way of doing this. No further record of the action should be kept; some organizations send the removed entries to the member of staff, so that they know the records have been removed from their files.

Appeals against disciplinary action

All disciplinary codes must have an inbuilt appeals procedure. Written appeals must be lodged within a period of time, usually within 7 working days of a decision, and are heard by someone in higher authority than the manager who dealt with the original case; appeals must normally be dealt with without delay, especially if it involves the dismissal of an employee or suspension without pay – in any case the process of a disciplinary case has an adverse affect on the morale of other staff and it is good practice to deal with the action and any appeal as efficaciously as possible. Appeal hearing proceedings follow the same lines as the disciplinary interview itself, except that on this occasion the line manager may be called as a witness to justify their original decision.

It must be emphasized that any disciplinary code relates to behaviour while at work; if an act of misconduct has not been committed at work you can consider whether such behaviour has breached the internal disciplinary code. Likewise, if a member of staff is either charged or convicted of a criminal offence, you must consider whether that offence or alleged offence calls for internal disciplinary action because of employment considerations. You are not required to wait for any external court decision before proceeding with internal disciplinary hearings if you feel this to be necessary.

Dismissal of a member of staff

In the UK, staff who have worked full time for at least 2 years continuously for the same employer, or part time for between at least 8 and 16 hours per week, continuously for at least 5 years, are protected by the Employment Protection (Consolidation) Act 1978, as amended, and can make a claim of unfair dismissal if their employer terminates their employment. Such employment protection laws are mirrored in other countries, although the precise details will vary from country to country. Wherever you operate, in cases of dismissal you must be able to show that you have acted fairly and reasonably. In the UK you cannot, for example, dismiss someone if they are exercising their rights in a connection with trade union activity, nor, as we have seen earlier, on the grounds of race, religion or sex; dismissal of a woman on the grounds of pregnancy is inadmissible. Even when you have the right to dismiss, for example if there is a statutory inability to do the job – that means that the law will be broken if the member of staff remains in post – you may consider that a better course of action would be to offer alternative employment should this be available.

When terminating the employment of a member of staff, say for lack of ability, if you have formal grievance and disciplinary codes it is vital to ensure that you have followed all the agreed procedures and that you have supporting documentation of the actions you have taken in the form of:

- Signed and dated notes of meetings
- Copies of letters of warning and evidence that these letters were in fact received by the employee
- Evidence that you have given the employee the time and opportunity to explain or improve; this may include providing training or counselling
- Evidence that you notified the person of their right of appeal.

What you regard as fair and reasonable may not be so interpreted by the industrial tribunal or a law court – for example, many cases are lost on technicalities because of failure to follow the correct procedures. You must be prepared to justify all your actions and the reasons for those actions; it must be clear that your behaviour was consistent and the person was not discriminated against or treated differently to other members of staff; for example, in cases involving disciplinary dismissal, did you adequately consider any mitigating circumstances?

According to UK employment laws, staff are entitled to receive a letter, within 14 days of requesting it, outlining the reasons for their dismissal – this letter may be used as evidence in a claim for unfair dismissal. Most employers, as a matter of good practice, automatically write to employees whose services are being terminated. Staff are entitled to receive the period of notice written into their contract and you are obliged to give the employee this period of notice or payment in lieu. Dismissal without notice should only happen when an employee has been found guilty under the agreed disciplinary code, of a very serious offence that warrants dismissal.

Normal periods of notice are 1 week, if on probation, rising to at least

12 weeks for a person employed by the same employer continuously for 12 years; the period of notice required from the employee on resignation may not be as long as this, but depends on whatever is written in the contract of employment. Both employer and employee can waive their rights to notice.

Termination on the grounds of frustration of contract

Frustration of contract occurs when, without default to the employer or the employee, it becomes either impossible or radically different for an employee to carry out the requirements of a contract due to an event which was not and could not be reasonably foreseen when the contract was drawn up. Examples of this occur when a member of staff is imprisoned or on long-term sick leave, and these cases it may be argued that the contract has been terminated on the grounds of frustration. However, in the case of long-term sickness or other possible cases of frustration which involve non-attendance at work, it would be wiser to approach the problem as a staff welfare matter, by counselling and other agreed consultative procedures.

Constructive dismissal

If an employee resigns of their own accord but is able to prove that they were forced out of the job, or that conditions were unbearable, they will be able to pursue a claim of constructive dismissal with an industrial tribunal. For example, trying to force an employee to resign, denigrating or ridiculing them, or changing their pay status or conditions of work without agreement, could all be construed as causing constructive dismissal.

How an industrial tribunal operates

Industrial tribunals are independent legal bodies set up in the UK to deal with a range of claims made by employees or former employees in relation to their employment rights. An industrial tribunal consists of a legally qualified chairman and two other people representing, respectively, employer and employee organizations. Employees who feel they have a case against their employer, such as unfair dismissal, have a legal right to pursue that case through the industrial tribunal procedures; precise instructions are published by the Department of Employment [7]. Most claims for unfair dismissal have to be made normally within a 3-month period of the termination, although later claims have been accepted, depending on the circumstances. Industrial tribunals also deal with claims of racial and sexual harassment, maternity rights and redundancy rights, but the time limits for submitting such claims can vary and need to be checked individually. In the UK, in most cases copies of the documents would be sent to an ACAS conciliation officer to see if settlements or agreements can be reached between the two parties before the tribunal hearing.

The whole purpose of the industrial tribunal system is to simplify the process of settling a dispute between an employer and an employee; costs are kept to a minimum. To this end, the proceedings are conducted in a straightforward and open manner although, as in any legal hearing, there is bound to be an element of stress for the people involved. Employers and employees can represent themselves or can be represented by a third party, for example an employee can be represented by a trade union official, and can call witnesses if necessary. Both parties are bound by the tribunal's decision; appeals can usually only be made on a point of law.

The tribunal will normally reach a decision at the end of the hearing. In reaching a decision in favour of the claimant, the tribunal will attempt to take into consideration their wishes; dismissed staff do not necessarily want their job back but may be seeking compensation from the employer. For example, in a case of proven unfair dismissal the tribunal will consider whether to make an order for re-instatement, re-engagement or compensation. Industrial tribunals operate at centres all over the UK and their proceedings are open to the public; there is usually no problem if you wish to see a tribunal in action, although it is wiser to telephone first if you wish to take a large number of people with you.

Advisory, Conciliation and Arbitration Service (ACAS)

ACAS is an independent body charged with the duty of promoting and improving industrial relations, and provides free services to all those concerned with any form of employment – employers, employees and trade union representatives. ACAS's best-known role is a conciliator or arbitrator in industrial disputes, but in fact a valuable service which needs to be stressed is their advisory role. ACAS has a number of public enquiry points to deal with enquiries about the legal rights and obligations of employers and employees, and ACAS advisors are available to offer practical assistance in a vast range of personnel matters, from the management of change to job design and work organization. ACAS also publishes a number of extremely helpful advisory handbooks and booklets, occasional papers and bibliographies. These are available free of charge from ACAS. In addition ACAS Codes of Practice can be purchased from HMSO.

References

1. American Library Association *Guidelines on job terminations for librarians and their employees*. Chicago: ALA
2. Ream, Betty (1987) *Enjoying retirement*, 9th rev. edn. London: The Industrial Society
3. *The IPM code of conduct for career and outplacement consultants*. (1991) London: IPM
4. Crofts, Pauline (1991) Helping people to face up to redundancy. *Personnel Management*, **23**(12), 24–27, 45.
5. Advisory, Conciliation and Arbitration Service (1988) *Redundancy handling*. London: ACAS
6. Advisory, Conciliation and Arbitration Service (1991) *Discipline at work: the ACAS advisory handbook*. London: ACAS
7. Department of Employment (1988) *Industrial tribunal proceedings*. London: HMSO

CHAPTER SIX

Communications, employee relations and staff welfare

Effective communication is a key factor in personnel work and in the management of any organization; to work properly, communications require commitment from the managers in the form of a communication policy, which includes a monitoring and review process to test the efficacy of any communication system used. We have already noted that, under the Companies Act 1985, organizations with more than 250 staff are required to provide staffing information relating to disabled employees in their directors' report; in addition, such companies are required to provide a statement about arrangements for communicating to employees matters that are likely to concern them, and in particular about the economic and financial performance of the company. Such legislation underlines the importance of effective communications to employees, which is equally important in small as well as in large organizations. Misinformation or reliance on rumour and gossip sounds the death knell for good employee relations. Informal methods of staff communication need to be consistent and promote the same message and information as the formal channels; if this does not happen the formal methods will be regarded with suspicion.

Oral methods of communication

It is good practice to establish a two-way system of communication so that information passes from the management level to all employees, and information and comments from the employees are passed to the managers. Depending on whether the communication process is for information, instruction or briefing, staff involvement and the opportunity to possibly influence management decisions leads to greater trust and commitment from the staff.

Formal methods of communication involving the cascading of information include briefing groups, in which the line managers regularly brief their staff and at the same time provide an opportunity for discussion and feedback on key issues and topics. This method works well when the line manager has strong leadership qualities, is committed to the system and is promoting an undistorted message. It will not work well if the line manager is not properly briefed and is unable to respond to questions and queries.

There are other formal channels of communication: regular meetings with employee representatives who are able to ask questions and seek clarification on issues, assist with the establishment of good industrial relations. These employee representatives have a responsibility in turn to relay to the staff the information received.

Staff meetings on a large scale can be effective where it is important to impart information about major organizational changes, but a two-way communication process is not generally achieved at such meetings – many staff feel intimidated by the occasion and consequently do not ask questions.

Written methods of communication

Written communications work well when the information is likely to be relevant for some time. These will include reports, memoranda, newsletters, staff journals and notices, including computerized message systems. These last are very effective for the rapid distribution of urgent information. The problem with written methods is that there is less opportunity for staff to ask questions or seek clarification; there is also a possibility that they may not fully understand the information. However, the advantages of using printed communications is that they can be circulated to all staff and retained for future reference. In distributing material for retention care must be taken that the information contained will remain valid for some time, or that it can be easily replaced if out of date. This is particularly pertinent, for example, to information in a staff handbook or the personnel manual.

Annual reports, which are largely intended for external consumption, can be used to acknowledge staff achievements and provide details on internal issues; a number of companies also now produce a separate annual report for employees. The use of notice boards remains a very popular method of communicating with staff; to be effective the notices should be attractively produced and the notice board will need regular weeding to remove out-of-date material.

Staff journals

The use of staff journals to promote information helps to establish a sense of organizational identity, but unless they are produced frequently they are not good vehicles for the rapid dissemination of information to staff; such journals usually concentrate on social and personnel achievements, or carry copy that will remain newsworthy for some time, such as health and safety advice. The editor will need to be provided with regular information about promotions, retirements and new appointees.

If you decide to have a staff journal you must be quite clear about editorial objectives and policy. Is it to reflect management policy or to be a truly independent voice of the staff? Matters such as cost, format, gathering copy, production and distribution will need to be carefully assessed if the final product is to be as professional as possible.

Letters to all staff

On major issues that concern all staff, letters can be sent to every employee. To retain impact, this is not a method that can be used frequently; to ensure that such a system does not undermine the line managers' credibility, they should be briefed in advance about such letters so that they will be in a position to answer staff questions.

It is important to bear in mind that no one system of communication should be used to the exclusion of all others. For communications to work effectively you will need to employ several of the above systems at the same time, for example backing up a staff briefing session by the circulation of a memorandum or notice.

Joining the professional association

It is essential for staff working in libraries and information services to belong to a professional association and the emergence of the concept of continuing professional development makes it strategically sensible to be in membership. Such associations represent the profession at international, national and local levels; they are a source of information and advice, enable you to keep up to date and prevent you from becoming professionally isolated. In the UK The Library Association is the largest professional organization for library and information services staff, and has regional branches and special interest groups. On joining The Library Association you are automatically enrolled in your local regional branch and can opt to join two special interest groups at no extra cost. If you wish to be kept up to date with personnel and training issues affecting library staff, you should opt to join the Personnel, Training and Education Group, which specializes in such issues.

The Library Association is concerned with standards of employment as well as education, staff training and continuing professional development. Many of its publications are issued free of charge and are listed in *Publications available from The Library Association* [1]. Of particular note is the newsletter *Employment News* [2] issued three times a year. Guidance notes available from the Employment and Resources Department cover specific LIS employment matters such as equal opportunities provision, job hunting, job sharing, violence in libraries and submitting regrading claims. The Education Department also issues a wide range of informative career leaflets. Further details about the benefits of joining can be obtained from the Membership Department. Membership is open to all categories of staff, whether in a professional or a supporting role.

Other organizations within the UK are the Institute of Information Scientists and Aslib, the Association for Information Management. Both these organizations are concerned with professional career development and the training of people working within the library and information field – the addresses of both organizations are at the end of this chapter.

In America, the American Library Association Office for Library Personnel Resources (OLPR) offers support and advice. OLPR issues *Library Personnel News* [3] which carries articles on a wide range of LIS-related issues, from legal questions on affirmative action to support staff issues, employee problems and a listing of new personnel literature of interest to LIS staff; as its name indicates, it is a useful source of information about personnel and staff development work in libraries. OLPR also produces 'Topics in Personnel' kits which provide guidance on a wide range of personnel issues – these contain reprints, original articles, sample forms and resource lists. They are widely used on courses dealing with library personnel management, continuing education workshops and by personnel officers in developing their policies. Topics include 'Career development: concepts and strategies', which deals with career development on behalf of the employer and the employee, the design of career development programmes and dealing with 'plateaued' employees. Other topics in this series of kits include such titles as *Help with performance appraisal, Help with the troubled employee, Administering staff cutbacks*, and *Pay equity – issues and strategy*. There is a charge for the above publications but other checklists and resource lists, such as the *Personnel materials checklist* and *Drug testing/ drug screening in the workplace*, are issued free of charge. The Special Libraries Association in the USA also does much work in management development and training for LIS staff. LIS professional associations worldwide are listed in *World guide to library, archival and information science associations* [4].

If your involvement with personnel and training is a large proportion of your work, you should consider joining the appropriate professional personnel/human resources organization, which can supply you with up-to-date relevant advice and information. The leading authority on human resource development in the British Isles is the Institute of Personnel Management. IPM have an extensive list of material suitable for both practitioners and students. IPM also runs an information library, with a postal service to members and a free telephone information service for members. Such professional support becomes all the more necessary if you are working in isolation and with little or no contact with professional human resource staff. In America the comparable organization is the Society for Human Resource Management; the address for this and for IPM are at the end of the book.

There are many other organizations concerned with human resource issues, some of which have already been mentioned. For example, organizations such as the Advisory, Conciliation and Arbitration Service have advisors available to offer practical assistance on human resource matters, as well as public enquiry points to deal with the legal rights and obligations of employers. The Industrial Society, founded in 1918, works with both employers and employees to develop good practice in involving people at work to increase the effectiveness of an organization. To this end the Industrial Society runs courses and conferences, carries out surveys and audits and produces books, videos and open training packages. There is also a library and information service, free to members, which contains examples of good working practice in employment matters. The Pepperell Department of the Industrial Society was originally specifically involved in women's training and development; this role has now been broadened to help develop individuals and organizations through the promotion of equality of opportunity in the workplace, in all areas of concern in equal opportunities, such as gender, race and disability. The British Institute of Management, the Institute of Directors and the Commission for Racial Equality are all organizations which are sources of information on human resource management and staff development matters.

Staff associations

Some organizations support and encourage the development of staff associations, which can be either purely social, or social and educational, or concern themselves with welfare issues. They are not to be confused with trade unions, whose functions are essentially quite different. Staff associations can greatly help with staff communications by the issue of a newsletter; the organization of social activities has a distinct advantage for the employer in terms of staff relationships and relaxation of departmental rivalries. The organization of educational activities, such as visits to other libraries or professional talks, will have the positive effect of enhancing opportunities for continuing development without the day-to-day involvement of the personnel and training staff, and provide the opportunity for interdepartmental training.

Staff association business is normally run by a committee of elected officials who work within a written constitution and byelaws; activities other than educational, normally take place outside working hours. Costs to the organization are usually minimal; you may need to provide access to telephones, postage, stationery, word processors and desktop publishers, particularly if a newsletter is being produced. Such 'costs' can be offset against improved morale and communication within the organization.

The role of the trade unions

On the national scene representatives of the trade unions have an important role to play in industrial democracy; the trade unions have representatives on many government advisory bodies concerned with the improvement of strategic issues affecting employees' overall job security and employment. Likewise, at local level the trade unions are concerned with improving employees' terms and conditions of employment; they are also concerned to protect and preserve jobs and ensure healthy and safe working practices in a safe working environment. Although there is no statutory right of union recognition in the UK, if a number of employees are members of a trade union they can request official recognition from an employer. Granting official recognition allows the union representatives to:

- Negotiate on behalf of members and have access to information for the purposes of collective bargaining. Such bargaining will affect the terms and conditions of work of the staff, and as such can eventually form part of the basic contract of employment.
- Take reasonable time off work for trade union duties and activities; for example, time to consult with a member of staff and to represent them at a disciplinary or industrial tribunal hearing, or time to attend a relevant union training course.
- Be consulted by the employer before redundancy procedures are effected, as outlined in Chapter 5.
- Receive information and consultation about the transfer of business, and sometimes rights to be recognized by a new employer; this includes measures that either the old or new employer intend to take concerning the staff.
- Have the right to appoint a safety representative; this also involves the right to participate in safety inspections at work.

The establishment and maintenance of a fair industrial relations climate is a major responsibility of the employer, and therefore of the manager. It is your responsibility and to your advantage to ensure good relations with staff representatives, and to develop informal as well as formal channels of communication. Regular joint consultative meetings between trade union representatives and management are one way of ensuring employees have the opportunity to participate in decision making which affects staff issues. Such meetings normally have a written constitution, a written agenda for each meeting and a reporting-back process for managers and employees alike. Such meetings should take place regularly; – at least once every 2 months is not unreasonable. Valuable as such formal meetings are, you should not underestimate the value of informal communications and pre-meeting briefings, so that real progress can be made at the formal meetings.

However, if you feel that there is not enough staff support for such recognition you can agree instead to representation rights, which basically entitles individual members of staff to be represented by a trade union official on occasions such as disciplinary hearings.

Developing negotiation skills

Negotiation is about coming to a mutually suitable agreement; it involves the ability to compromise, to give as well as take, in order to bring about a solution to a problem. The objectives of negotiation are discussed by Pratt and Bennett *Elements of personnel management* [5] who state that successful negotiation requires skill, preparation and a great deal of experience. Most important is the time spent in preparing for negotiation and in deciding on your strategy.

If you become involved in a trade union negotiation about terms and conditions of work you must learn to:

- Identify the primary and secondary aims of the trade union and what their bargaining position might be: sometimes claims or proposals are set high to allow room for manoeuvre; for this reason it is also important to try to ascertain what real expectations they have of the claim or proposal being met – your bargaining hand will be strengthened if these expectations are low. The use of informal meetings can greatly assist in this process.
- Appraise the claim/proposal and develop your own strategy to meet or overturn it, or to put forward an alternative. This means examining and costing the claim/proposal in detail and knowing what you can and cannot afford to do in terms of accepting or rejecting it. You may decide to accept the claim in return for agreement to change other conditions. Whatever your final strategy, you should never reveal your 'bottom line' position and you must be prepared to make concessions in order to reach a reasonable agreement.

Health and safety at work

The major legislation affecting health and safety at work in the UK is the Health and Safety at Work Act 1974. Under this Act the workplace is liable to inspection from either the Health and Safety Executive, which is a government body attached to the Department of Employment, or the local authority, and both these organizations have the power to prosecute or insist on changes to improve health and safety matters. Other legislation that affects safety at work is the Factories Act 1961 and the Offices, Shops and Railways Act 1963; this latter Act deals mainly with standards of heating, lighting and the provision of facilities such as hot and cold water. The Reporting of Injuries, Diseases and Dangerous Occurrences Regulations, 1985, affect the procedures to be followed when reporting accidents that occur in offices.

The Health and Safety at Work Act sets out clearly the individual responsibilities of employers, managers and members of staff in relation to health and safety at work; it differs from other legislation in that individual members of staff assume responsibility as well as the employer, and as individuals can be prosecuted for serious breaches of the Act. The law requires employers to provide all employees with training and information about health and safety matters and their responsibilities while at work to their colleagues, the public and themselves. Many commercial multimedia training packages are now available to assist employers to meet this requirement. Employees are required to take reasonable care at work, both of themselves and others who could be affected by what they do; to this end they must not interfere with or misuse anything provided in the interests of health and safety. By law they must cooperate with their employer to enable that employer to carry out their responsibilities under the Act. The overall purpose of the Act is to ensure that everyone at work is totally safety-conscious.

The Act states that any employer of more than five people must have a written policy covering health and safety, and most employers now issue statements of safety policy at an early stage of an employee's appointment; these outline the responsibilities of every individual, from the managing director to the newest recruit, and will include details of any joint consultative arrangements with staff representatives for health and safety matters. If special hazards have been identified, the employer is required to issue codes of safe working practices; these would normally cover the use of dangerous equipment or chemicals.

The Act also obliges the regular monitoring of health and safety standards, which can be done in cooperation with safety representatives appointed by the trade union. The employer is required to provide a safe and healthy place of work and safe plant, equipment and systems. The regular monitoring of standards is best done with the assistance of a checklist which enables health and safety items to be systematically checked and reported upon. Questions for inclusion on such a checklist would be:

- Are fire escapes free from obstruction?
- Is fire-fighting equipment in working order?
- Are fire security doors shut?
- Are emergency exit routes clearly marked?
- Are floor surfaces and stairs in a safe condition?
- Is the library in a clean and tidy condition?
- Is the heating/ventilation adequate?
- Are electrical fittings/wiring in a safe condition?
- Are there any trailing wires likely to cause accidents?
- Do all the light switches work and is the lighting adequate for working conditions?
- Are any chemicals/cleaning fluids safely kept and properly labelled?
- Is the first-aid box correctly stocked and its location clearly marked?
- Is all the equipment/furniture in safe working order?
- Are trolleys provided for staff to move heavy books/equipment?
- Are all the staff adequately trained in safe working practices and their responsibilities for health and safety at work?
- Is there adequate provision for the security of staff and their possessions?

This list is not meant to be comprehensive but to act as a guide to compiling a safety inspection checklist suitable for your own library. Each section will need careful consideration to itemize potential risks and hazards for regular checking. To analyse how you can further enhance each section, a sample of some of the safety rules in the use of electrical appliances compiled by the City of Newcastle upon Tyne Leisure Services Department [6] is reproduced here:

Safety Rules in the use of Electrical Appliances

Flexible Cable: check that the cable is connected firmly at both the appliance and the plug, i.e. that the outer sheathing of the cable is held in the grips provided.

Check that the cable is free from kinks and is not damaged, i.e. is free from cuts, scuffing, burns, fraying, etc., to ensure that the inner wires are not exposed.

Plug: Check for damage, i.e. cracks or breakage.

Check for signs of overheating, i.e. scorch marks on plug body or cover.

Socket outlets: Check for damage, i.e. cracks, breakage, exposed wires or metal parts.

Check for signs of overheating, i.e. scorch marks.

Check that sockets are secured firmly to the wall or trunking, as appropriate.

Appliance: Check that the case or cover is not damaged and is fixed securely.

Check that the on/off switch is not damaged and works correctly.

Such complete and comprehensive instructions leave no doubt about the function and the operation of a safety inspection. Employers are required to take action to resolve any situations that are found to be hazardous. This may mean anything from the urgent replacement or repair of equipment to major or minor building maintenance – provision of the finance to ensure health and safety standards is a management responsibility.

Safety committees

Employers are required to consult with staff to develop a coordinated approach to health and safety at work. This can be done by the establishment of safety committees to promote cooperation between employer and employees. In large organizations these committees are able to take an overall view of reports made by safety representatives and assist in the development of safety rules and regulations and safety training. Such a committee is in a good position to monitor any accidents, near accidents, dangerous incidents or occurrences at work, and to recommend corrective action to prevent further incidents.

Regular safety inspections do not necessarily reveal all potential problems. For this reason it is important to set up a system of monitoring accidents or near accidents, to help identify potential problems. If, for example, people are always falling down the same flight of stairs, investigations might reveal faulty lighting, a dangerous, broken or slippery floor surface, an insecure handrail, litter, dirt or obstructions which had not been cleared away, or a lack of warning notices.

An example of the constitution for a health and safety committee is included here from the Westminster City Libraries Health and Safety Policy Statement [7]:

Safety Committee Objectives

To promote cooperation between employer and employees in instigating, developing and carrying out measures to ensure the health and safety at work of employees

Functions

1. To consider reports of accidents and identify particular trends and recommend corrective action

2. To examine safety audit reports on a similar basis

3. To consider reports and factual information provided by the Health and Safety Executive as the enforcing authority under the Act

4. To consider reports which safety representatives may wish to submit

5. To assist in the development of safety rules and safe systems of work

6. To comment on the safety content of employee training

7. To comment on the adequacy of safety and health communication and publicity in the work place

---

8. To provide as required a link with the appropriate inspectorates of the Health and Safety Executive as the enforcing authority

Conduct of the Meetings

Frequency and venue to be determined by the Committee.

Fire precautions

One of the issues the safety committees will consider as a matter of priority will be the arrangement for fire prevention, precautions and evacuation of the building in the event of a fire alarm. In the UK the Fire Precautions Act 1971 requires that all premises where there are more than 20 people, or in which more than 10 people are employed, other than on the ground floor, must have a fire certificate – application for these must be made to the local Fire Authority. Before a fire certificate is issued the Fire Authority will request information about the building, fire escape routes and related safety matters.

All staff need to be aware of the fire instructions, or instructions for dealing with bomb threats for the building in which they work, and must be trained to comply with such instructions. Normally most organizations post fire instructions in prominent places, with details of exit routes and assembly points outside the building. Staff need to be trained in prompt action to report a fire or smoke, and some staff will be trained in the use of fire extinguishers.

People working in libraries and information centres will be responsible for the evacuation of users as well as for themselves. All staff must be conversant with the evacuation procedures and be aware of emergency exit routes, particularly if they are dealing with children, the elderly or people with disabilities who might need assistance to leave the building safely. To monitor the effectiveness of these evacuation procedures you should arrange for periodic fire drills – not just the testing of fire bells which, if fitted, must be tested once a week – but the total evacuation of the building. The Fire Precautions Act 1971 recommends quarterly fire drills; one a year is the minimum. If your staff turnover is high you may need to organize more frequent drills, such as every 6 months. To be really effective, fire drills should take place unexpectedly but this may not be totally possible if you intend to monitor the evacuation. At the most, staff should be aware that a fire evacuation drill will happen on a certain date, but to preserve the element of surprise necessary to test the efficacy of the procedures, the time should not be revealed. To cause as little disruption as possible fire drills could be scheduled to take place either before the public arrive or after they leave.

You will need to check:

- The time the evacuation took and whether it was satisfactory
- That everyone knew what to do and did it; staff must stop whatever they are doing immediately, and leave the building by the nearest exit using the stairs and not the lift/elevator
- That the fire alarm was heard all over the building
- That a nominated fire officer had checked that offices and toilets/ cloakrooms were empty
- That everyone assembled at the right place and had been accounted for.

First aid

First aid at work is covered by the Health and Safety (First Aid) Regulations, which came into force in the UK in 1981, together with an approved Code of Practice; both were subsequently updated and revised in 1990. The aim of the regulations is to ensure that all people at work are adequately covered by first-aid provision. Under these regulations an employer has a duty to provide equipment, facilities and trained personnel as adequate and appropriate to ensure that first aid can be given to employees if they become ill or have an accident at work. As part of the health and safety procedures all employees need to know where the first-aid box is kept – it should be easily accessible. The contents of the first-aid box will vary according to the number of staff at the location; the required contents are laid down by the Health and Safety (First Aid) Regulations mentioned above. Under these regulations, in libraries or organizations with under 50 staff, you will need to designate one person to ensure that the contents are regularly checked and replenished after use; a contents list kept inside the box will facilitate this. This same appointed person will be responsible for reporting accidents and dangerous incidents, including any action taken and by whom. These regulations affect first aid for the staff only and do not apply to library users; the regulations change if staffing number exceed 50 people.

Under these same regulations the appointed person will be responsible for emergency first-aid treatment, for which they must have had training; they are also required to take charge of any emergency involving staff illness or accidents. Many employers provide properly certificated first-aid training for staff and try to have at least one properly trained and certificated first-aider in each department. However, it is acknowledged that this is unlikely to ensure that a trained first-aider is always on duty for all public sector library opening hours: it is only if there is a high degree of risk that the regulations require at least one trained and certificated first-aider to be appointed. Certificated first-aid courses are run reasonably cheaply by organizations such as the Red Cross or St. John Ambulance. These provide training and testing of first-aiders and offer refresher courses to people whose certificates are about to expire; a certificate is valid for 3 years. Some employers also pay a small salary supplement to certificated first-aiders. If a decision is taken to have a certificated first-aider at each library/location, a register will need to be maintained to ensure coverage and to trigger a reminder about renewal courses before any certificate expires.

When possible, employers should try to provide first-aid or sick rooms for staff who are taken ill while at work. Not all employers have the facilities to do this, but a good employer will ensure that a quiet place can be set aside for such staff; the provision of pillows and blankets will also help to keep the person warm and as comfortable as possible until they feel better or until proper medical help arrives. The provision of a sickroom is not a requirement if there are fewer than 250 staff in one location.

Although all the above guidelines refer to legislation in the UK, the effect of the working practices associated with this legislation has been to develop effective measures to ensure the health and safety of all people at work; these working practices can provide a case study framework which can be amended or altered to apply to local working conditions and employment practices in other countries; however, it will always be important to verify the precise health and safety legislation requirements of the country in which you work.

Codes of safe working practice

As mentioned above, the Health and Safety at Work Act 1974 requires employers to issue codes of safe working practices. Obviously in areas of work such as leisure centres or in grounds maintenance there will be a need for many such codes, since employees in those occupations regularly handle toxic chemicals and dangerous plant and equipment.

Security and the use of visual display units are two areas in library and information work where it is important to have codes of safe working practice.

Security of buildings and property

A code for safe working practice concerning security is essential. This will outline the best security procedures, for example in opening and closing a building, security of equipment and personal property and the importance of checking on visitors and external maintenance workers who may appear in the library. Most organizational representatives now carry identity cards, and visitors to large organizations are also issued with permits or temporary visitor's cards for security purposes; you should not be afraid to ask to see them nor to refuse access if one cannot be produced; without being discourteous, a simple telephone call can nearly always sort out who has the right to be in the building and who has not.

Security of personal information

Security is also a matter relating to personal information about employees, such as their home telephone number and address. This information must be held in a secure location, with the right of access limited to known people. Before any confidential information can be disclosed you must check the enquirer's identity, status and their 'right to know'. Personal information about staff should never be divulged to any enquirer without first checking with the individual concerned; an effective way to deal with this is to offer to give a message to the employee from the enquirer; it will then be up to the employee to contact the enquirer if they so wish.

Written requests for references normally come on headed notepaper from an organization; hopefully, although not always, the member of staff will have already asked you to act as a referee. Requests for telephone references can be more suspect. It is better never to deal with these immediately unless you know it is a bona fide call; ask for the name of the organization and offer to ring the caller back – check that the number you have been asked to ring is in fact correct for the information you have been given.

Security of staff

Violence and aggression in society at large expose library staff, often working in library buildings, late at night, to unacceptable situations. Problems can be alleviated, though not totally resolved, by providing training in defusing violent and aggressive situations; this training may also include an element of self-defence, but staff must be made aware of differences between genuine self-defence and possible charges of initiating an assault. Most public organizations now have policies regarding procedures if staff are assaulted; these also outline the policy regarding prosecution of offenders, and insurance matters. Persistent violence at one location is obviously a matter for the police, but preventive measures such as better lighting, security/panic buttons to call assistance, and a change of opening hours may help to reduce the problem. Staff working late at night should ideally never be on duty on their own in an isolated location. The Library Association publishes a leaflet [8] which outlines a preventive framework; it also contains advice about handling aggressive incidents.

The Citizen's Charter [9], which is a UK government White Paper to encourage quality public services, states that public servants will be expected to wear name badges and give their names in telephone and letter communication. The Charter does have an exception clause which exempts staff who might be putting themselves at risk by doing so – this has obvious implications for library staff who, by wearing name badges in some situations or locations, could expose themselves to sexual or other forms of harassment; identification of a member of staff by name can easily lead to identification of their home address, leading to unwanted personal telephone calls and other forms of harassment. In these cases badges identifying someone as a member of staff would be sufficient to promote the 'user-friendly' concept.

Safe working practices for VDU use

The continued growth in the use of visual display units, which has radically reformed the working practices of most library and information staff, has led to the development of codes of safe working practice for employees who use them, although all available evidence suggests that the risks from continued use of VDUs are very low. Staff who work for long periods at VDU terminals have complained of tiredness to the eyes, body fatigue, headaches and back and neck strain. Repetitive strain injury is now an accepted problem associated with the constant use of keyboards, particularly for word-processor operators.

Good ergonomic planning, design and positioning of workstations, seating, lighting and ventilation can go a long way to resolving potential problems. It is recognized that employees who are engaged in constant concentrated work at a VDU terminal must have a break of at least 10 minutes in every hour, or 20 minutes in every 2-hour period; short frequent breaks are more satisfactory than longer but more infrequent breaks – if possible it is much better to design the job so that there are natural breaks while other work is completed.

Staff who wear spectacles or contact lenses should consult an optician before starting to use a VDU: in fact it is good health practice to advise all staff to have an eye test before they start to use a VDU terminal. Many employers send staff for such tests and if necessary contribute towards the cost of spectacles if these are required for such work. Staff should also be made aware that some minor tranquillizers and other psychoactive drugs do produce occasional side effects which affect the eyes and mimic visual fatigue. Although the risk is very low, people who suffer from photosensitive epilepsy may also experience problems in the use of VDUs, caused by the flickering of the screen.

There is still much dispute about the effects of VDU radiation on pregnancy; pregnant women should be given the option of not working consistently on a VDU terminal. The main problem may not be radiation but body stress, and if possible women should be given other work to do or a variety of work to help alleviate the problem.

The Health and Safety Commission states that there are currently no legislative requirements applying specifically to VDU work, although guidelines have been issued [10,11]. At the time of writing, draft regulations have also been issued [12], which are intended to implement European Directive 90/270/EEC on the minimum safety and health requirements for work with display screen equipment, but the finalized regulations will not be issued until full consultation with all interested parties has taken place. The Directive makes a number of proposals, for example requiring employers to ensure that staff who become VDU users have the right to appropriate eye and eyesight tests, to provide appropriate health and safety training and to plan routines so that the user's work is periodically interrupted. The Directive also requires every employer to analyse the workstation in order to analyse the risk to the health and safety of the user. A number of other health and safety directives are also under consideration, including one dealing with health and safety requirements for the workplace. The Health and Safety Commission recognize that, as a result of negotiations at Community level, compromises which will require changes and additions to the UK Health and Safety legislation will need to be made, although it is hoped not to disrupt the existing basic structure of the Health and Safety at Work Act.

Smoking policies

Smoking has always been banned in the public parts of UK libraries; it is now becoming more and more common to find that this non-smoking policy has been extended to the non-public areas as well. The Health and Safety at Work Act requires the employer to provide a safe and healthy working environment: this is now seen to include the provision of a smoke-free atmosphere. Passive smoking is regarded as a health hazard for non-smokers, particularly for pregnant women, for whom there are special risks, and a recent law case in the UK allowed that an employee who had an abnormally sensitive reaction had suffered personal injury at work by being forced to inhale tobacco smoke. Indeed, in the USA some organizations refuse to employ people who smoke, even if they do not actually do so at work.

Proposing a non-smoking policy is an issue that can cause conflict if not carefully handled. It is certainly a matter that should be considered by the safety committee and safety representatives, and their assistance sought to encourage its adoption; a total no-smoking ban can be avoided by agreeing places where smokers can go to smoke, although smoking is normally banned from all communal areas. In all events it is important to have consulted the staff in advance of the introduction of a smoking policy, with a promise to review its operation after a period of time. The Institute of Personnel Management publish a concise guide to introducing a smoking policy [13] which makes it clear that the issue is not about *whether* people smoke but *where* they smoke while at work.

Stress at work

Stress affects people in very different ways. Positive stress will stimulate staff to increase their activity in order to meet a particular challenge, and a certain amount of positive stress is healthy and necessary. Negative stress produces fatigue and exhaustion, and prolonged negative stress will most definitely affect an employee's ability to work effectively. Stress may reveal itself in a number of ways – by absenteeism, lateness, irritability, and inability to meet targets or poor performance. Your role is to try to help the employee identify the cause of the stress and to try to resolve that cause. Non-productive stress may be caused by job design or management style, and you may be able to resolve these problems. Organizational changes which cause anxiety and apprehension are another source of stress at work; Geoff White of the Work Research Unit of ACAS outlines strategies for reducing pressures during change in his paper *Managing stress in organisational change* [14]. However, stress need not be permanent nor necessarily caused by work environment: domestic problems are just as responsible for causing stress which affects the employee at work. Counselling staff who are suffering from stress may help them to identify the cause of the problem and to develop techniques to deal with it. Courses which deal with stress management will help the employee to recognize stress signals for themselves, and will help them overcome stressful situations. DeCarlo and Gruenfeld [15] identify the two basic approaches to corporate stress management – rehabilitation and prevention. Under rehabilitation, stress levels are allowed to build up until the work performance of the member of staff is badly affected, at which stage some form of rehabilitation is offered in the form of guidance or counselling. Far more important, as they emphasize, is a prevention programme aimed at eliminating unnecessary stress from the workplace, to examine and revise the debilitating aspects of the work culture; linked to this is the promotion of healthier lifestyles, in and outside work, which greatly increase employees' ability to cope with stressful situations.

Staff health and welfare

Some organizations have policies relating to the overall health and wellbeing of staff. This will include allowing women time off for breast and cervical cancer screening, and monitoring the health of staff by measures such as blood pressure checks; included here will be policies to encourage healthy eating. Along with non-smoking policies many organizations now also have a complete alcohol ban during working hours. Lunchtime drinking causes a decrease in efficiency in the afternoons, and alcohol abuse is the direct cause of much absenteeism and sick leave and a strain on the remaining members of the staff who have to work harder to cover for the absent employee. As with stress, the employee who has an alcohol problem may be first noticed – though not always – through general poor performance, unreliability or bad relations with colleagues. Not all staff who abuse alcohol will have the obvious signs of blurred speech or impaired concentration.

If you have already invested a great deal of time and money in training and development of the employee, it is better to tackle the problem initially by counselling and agreeing a plan of action to overcome the problem; this could involve the employee seeking professional help. This is a situation that will need to be monitored, but if it fails you will have no alternative but to turn to the disciplinary code. The Department of Employment has produced guidelines for employers who wish to introduce a policy on the use of alcohol, which gives practical advice on how to implement and monitor such a policy [16]. They have also published a similar guide which focuses on the use of illegal drugs [17]. As this guide rightly point out, illegal drugs, as well as alcohol abuse, become a workplace problem as they affect safety, job performance and productivity. The guide examines recognition of a drug-related problem in staff and examines how to implement and monitor any policy.

Staff welfare can be the poor relation in the implementation of the requirements of the Health and Safety at Work Act. The physical welfare of staff is generally well looked after, but traditionally the stress-related matters and those of emotional and psychological well-being are not so often addressed. Matters such as stress, smoking, drug abuse and alcohol, which affect the performance of staff at work are all matters of increasing importance to employers. Providing a welfare counselling service, or simply being available to talk to staff who, for whatever reason, need to talk, will help improve employee relations and make staff at work more effective.

References

1. Library Association. *Publications available from the Library Association*. London: Library Association
2. Library Association (1991) *Employment News*. London: Library Association, Employment and Resources Department
3. American Library Association (1987) *Library Personnel News*. Chicago: Office for Library Personnel Resources
4. Fang, J. R. and Songe, A. (1990) *World guide to library, archival information science associations*. Munich: K. G. Saur
5. Pratt, K. J. and Bennett, S. G. (1989) *Elements of personnel management*, 2nd edn. London: Van Nostrand-Reinhold
6. City of Newcastle upon Tyne Leisure Services Department (1991) *Corporate guidance to all employees on the safe use of electrical appliances*.
7. Westminster City Libraries (1979) *Health and safety policy statement*.
8. Library Association (1987) *Violence in libraries: preventing aggressive and unacceptable behaviour in libraries. Advice to Members*. London: The Library Association
9. Cabinet Office (1991) *Citizen's charter*. Government White Paper Cm. 1599. London: HMSO
10. Health and Safety Executive (1983) *Visual display units*. London: HMSO
11. Health and Safety Executive (1991) *Working with VDUs*. London: HMSO
12. Health and Safety Commission (1992) *Work with display screen equipment: proposals for regulations and guidance*. Consultative Document. London: HSE
13. Institute of Personnel Management (1990) *Smoking policies at work: an IPM guide*. London: IPM
14. White, Geoff (1984) *Managing stress in organisational change*. Work Research Unit Occasional Paper No. 31. London: ACAS
15. DeCarlo, Donald T. and Gruenfeld, Deborah H. (1989) *Stress in the American workplace: alternatives for the working wounded*. Pennsylvania: LRP Publications
16. Department of Employment (1991) *Alcohol in the workplace: a guide for employers*. London: HMSO
17. Department of Employment (1990) *Drug misuse in the workplace: a guide for employers*. London: HMSO

PART TWO

The management of staff training and development

Sylvia P. Webb

CHAPTER SEVEN

The structure and purpose of staff development

Staff training and development is a key area for any librarian or information manager. For the service to operate effectively, library and information staff need to be seen not merely as signposts to sources, but rather as the key to their effective use and exploitation, that is, as professional information handlers and organizers who are also good communicators. Today's multimedia information-dependent society presents numerous opportunities for those working in LIS to be involved in a range of activities across the organization in which they work. For example, the information department of a legal or accounting practice could easily be involved in a range of IT (information technology) developments across the firm, such as the setting up of internal databases and records management systems, as well as in other company-wide activities such as marketing and PR. In public libraries there has been a considerable increase in the setting up of new or specialist services and departments, for example the introduction of public-access IT-based services such as OPACs or CD-ROMs; or of fee-based business information services. In both these examples, attitudes and skills as well as specialist knowledge are crucial. There are also services which operate off-site, taking information out to particular areas of the community, for example to prisons or to the housebound. Both private sector companies and local authorities are being called upon to streamline procedures and become more cost-effective, introducing more value-added services, for which charges are increasingly likely to be made to the ultimate user of the information. All these activities require a variety of skills and knowledge over and above basic information-seeking and finding skills – which are in themselves becoming more complex, yet at the same time more exciting given the range of sources and formats now available, including the ability to manipulate data as well as store it.

Already the few examples given above will have indicated numerous possible areas for training and development, but in addition to skills and knowledge there is another vital objective: that of raising staff morale and motivation, something which underpins the whole service. If morale is low and motivation lacking in just one member of staff, it quickly reflects on the service as a whole. All types of library and information service benefit from the encouragement and support of training and development, but it must be carefully planned and structured, and available to staff at all levels. Before going any further it might be useful to mention the difference between training and development, although they are closely linked. Training is usually considered to be the process through which job-related skills are achieved, yet at the same time it is itself part of the broader process of an individual's development, the latter being concerned with attitudes, motivation, increased awareness and personal qualities. Training could perhaps be regarded as a series of short clearly defined modules, whereas development is a lifelong process contributing to personal as well as work-related advancement.

Each time a new member of staff is appointed, a new personality with a variety of experience, knowledge, interests and skills is brought into the organization. As the departmental manager you will want to help that person to build on those, and in so doing, enhance both the service and the job. However, your involvement will not only benefit the individual and the service: the process of training and developing your staff will also be instrumental in your own personal development.

Libraries and information services operate within a whole range of organizational settings: they may be part of a public library service within a local authority or form a central part of the educational process, for example within a university. Government departments, both central and local, also have large collections of information, as do hospitals, charities and voluntary organizations, industrial and commercial firms, professional and trade associations. The organizational objectives may be very different, as may be the way in which information is used and perceived. Different information needs may be satisfied in different ways, but there will be certain core areas of information organization and handling which will be common to all. The key factors likely to dictate the direction and style of information provision and exploitation are, first, the objectives that need to be met by the organization, and secondly, the organizational culture, for example the hierarchy, structure, norms and procedures that exist. These will all need to be considered when setting out to establish a training and development policy for the library or information department, which may itself be part of another broader function such as research or education. This is quite common in the private sector, as demonstrated in a research study [1] which looked at 65 business organizations and revealed that in almost half of them LIS formed part of another department – marketing, computer services, research or consultancy. It could also be the case that the LIS has other functions as part of its overall portfolio; for example, information services may include responsibility for records management, database development or IT training. Having talked about such diversity in terms of the private sector, it must be said that there are just as many different LIS roles in the public sector, for example in public libraries there are youth libraries, music and drama collections, local history archives, reference, business and commercial services. Another notable difference between public libraries and special libraries is that in the public library setting the organization will have within it a large number of library/information staff, whereas in an industrial or commercial firm, however large the library/information service may be, the LIS staff will always be very much in a minority. This is something of which the manager needs to be very aware in terms of the possible differences in organizational understanding and perception of the capability of LIS staff, and the way in which that could influence support for their training and development. This therefore forms a key part of the development process that managers themselves need to pursue, i.e. acquiring an understanding of the organization and the skills to ensure that that understanding is put to maximum use in developing the full potential of the individual and the service to meet the organization's objectives.

All these factors will influence the type of training activity that you will want and need to put into place, and the personal qualities that individuals will require to be effective in their particular role. Throughout Part Two current practice is illustrated by case studies. Examples quoted from management and professional literature are also used to demonstrate ways in which training and development activities can be structured and managed. Case studies include international, national

and locally based organizations. The first of these shows the importance of integrating specialist training into the organization's overall
training programme.

Case study: The British Council

The British Council, when planning training for its library and information staff, literally has to think globally, having around 90 offices and
6500 staff in countries throughout the world. The aim of the British
Council is to promote Britain abroad and to provide access to British
ideas, talents and experience in education and training, books and
periodicals, the English language, the arts, the sciences and technology.
Among its services each office provides a library and information
service to local enquirers seeking answers to questions about almost
anything to do with life in Britain, with a considerable number of these
enquirers seeking details about various aspects of British education.
Enquiries may come from government offices, local universities and
other organizations, or from interested individuals. The Libraries Books
and Information Division (LIBID) at the headquarters of the British
Council in Manchester is responsible for designing and running a series
of specific training events for different levels of LIS staff, covering a
range of subjects and using a variety of teaching methods and
materials. However, the development of training for all divisions is
carried out in conjunction with the central training department and as
part of the British Council's overall management and development
programme, MANDATE.

MANDATE was introduced in 1991 and staff were familiarized with
the concept through the circulation of a well set-out leaflet describing
the programme and its benefits. Sections of this are reproduced below
with kind permission of the British Council.

What is Mandate?

- Mandate stands for Management Training and Development Exercise
- Mandate provides training and development services required by
  managers and their staff to achieve corporate objectives
- Mandate's services are shaped by the Council's priorities
- Mandate gives you the opportunity to improve your skills and
  develop your career

What are the benefits?

Mandate benefits you, your line manager and the Council because it:
- meets direct needs and is job-related
- fosters personal development and professionalism
- gives a sense of direction to training and development
- increases effectiveness and efficiency
- improves communication
- improves morale
- supports key changes
- gives an organizational focus to development
- attracts and keeps good staff

How Mandate helps you:
- The programmes are developmental: you are able to undertake further training in key skills as you move jobs or through the grades
- The programmes are flexible: you do the training when you and your line manager feel that you need it
- The programmes are innovative and you learn in many different ways: open learning, courses and workshops, computer-based training, projects, attachments and job-swaps
- The training modules will be offered regularly in the UK and in two designated Regional Training Centres in Egypt and India

Other services that Mandate provides:
- Specialist advice to help line managers identify training needs and strategies
- Specific training for work units and projects
- Full-time or short-term external training where appropriate
- Customized Professional Training Programmes (for individuals or groups) to update specialist knowledge and skills
- A Management Qualifications Programme using distance learning and leading to the Certificate or Diploma in Management
- Training for trainers: those who have responsibility in work units for training other staff
- A Further Education Scheme to support personal development, particularly for junior staff
- Language training and cultural orientation to prepare UK staff for an overseas posting

[The leaflet also shows the core Mandate programmes with a chart grouping the training modules by skill area and type of course, the names of the training team responsible for each type of programme, and a list of the specialist training and development advisers who have been assigned to each division.]

The Libraries Books and Information Division (LIBID) runs a number of specialist programmes for staff worldwide, some with English as a first language and many with a different mother tongue; both with and without LIS qualifications. The subjects covered range from book promotion and information provision to information technology and library and information services management. Course development has been very much as a response to feedback, particularly from overseas participants who have attended previous courses. Details are circulated to all offices worldwide and course descriptions, especially in terms of the aims and level, have to be clearly stated in order that those wishing to apply have all the information necessary to help them make the most appropriate choice. Because of the complexity of getting people from around the world together for a course, training events have to be planned well in advance and programmes scheduled to allow overseas visitors to take the opportunity to arrange other commitments during their stay. Those running British Council courses need to take particular account of cultural differences, for example the accepted use and form of personal names, and special learning requirements of delegates e.g. in terms of language. Training materials, especially handouts and work-books, play an important part, offering delegates the chance to re-read those sections of the programme where they require better understanding, and giving them something to take back to the workplace for future reference.

This first chapter and the case study illustrate the numerous considerations for any LIS manager seeking to review the training and development opportunities for, and needs of, their staff. It also emphasizes the benefits to both the individual and the service of viewing such activities in an organizational context.

References

1. Webb, S. P. (1991) *Best practice?: continuing professional development for library/information staff in UK professional firms.* British Library R & D Report 6039. Berkhamsted: Sylvia P. Webb.

CHAPTER EIGHT

Assessing training needs

A useful starting point in assessing training needs could be to review the service itself to establish its main thrust and to see what changes need to be made, for example, in providing current awareness services, or setting up a business information service. These would certainly require in the first case a keen awareness of the employing organization's constantly changing activities and its plans for the future, as well as communication skills and the ability to select the most appropriate medium for its delivery, e.g. disseminating information in hard-copy form as a printed bulletin or via electronic mail, according to the norms and procedures which seem to operate most successfully in responding to organizational needs. In the second case, that of setting up a business information service, an understanding of the business environment, its language and how it operates, plus the ability to work to tight deadlines and retain the enquirer's confidence would be essential.

As the British Council case study in the previous chapter suggests, in assessing training needs there will be across-the-board organizational considerations and more specific departmental requirements. In considering the organization as a whole, one might start by asking such questions as:

- Is there a central training function?
- What is the overall policy towards training?
- Is there a career structure in place?
- Are there any internal guidelines for managers to follow, for example in conducting appraisals as part of the development process or in evaluating training?

- Is there an organizational staff manual setting out, among other things, training and development practices and procedures?
- What has the organization already promised the individual in the letter of offer?
- What expectations were set at the interview stage?

On a departmental basis the following types of question would need to be asked:

- What has already taken place, perhaps on an ad hoc basis, within the department?
- Are you able to support the requirements of the library/information professional associations in terms of either the qualification process, or continuing professional development?
- How do these fit into the organizational framework?

The way in which such questions were addressed by a Scottish public library service provides an excellent model, as set out below.

Case study: Glasgow City Libraries – I

Glasgow City Libraries Training and Development Plan
City of Glasgow District Council
Personnel Department
Formulating a Departmental Training Plan
Notes for Guidance

1. *Introduction*
It is Council policy that each Department will produce an annual Training Plan and that this shall be submitted to the Director of Personnel for approval. The following 'Notes for Guidance' have been compiled to assist Heads of Department and those responsible for co-ordinating departmental training and development requirements, who may wish to adopt a more structured approach to the planning and forecasting of training and development activities within their departments.

2. *Benefits of a Training Plan*
The formulation of a Training Plan should result in the following benefits.
  (i) The training and development needs of employees are identified and catered for in a structured manner, through a systematic

analysis of what is required. Factors which would be considered in carrying out such an analysis would include:

- current and future job requirements
- maintaining or improving the performance of employees within their jobs
- employees with potential
- any special needs of groups or individual employees, arising from, for example, technological change, re-organization or the introduction of new procedures within the department
- needs arising from the Council's Staff Assessment and Development Scheme. [See Chapter 10]

(ii) The training and development needs of employees are seen as an integral part of the department's short and medium term aims and objectives, thereby ensuring the training and development of employees makes a positive contribution to departmental activities.

(iii) The persons responsible for the training and development of employees within a department are clearly identified and levels of accountability defined.

(iv) A record is provided of the training and development activities carried out by a department as a whole, creating the basis for reviewing the effectiveness of training and allocating future resources.

(v) It demonstrates an active commitment to the training and development of employees within a department in line with the Council's overall 'Training Policy'.

3. *Conducting the Analysis*

Generally speaking training and development needs may arise either from key strategic or operational issues facing the Department or from individual job needs. Gathering the information on what is required for the coming year can be carried out by a variety of methods. These range from detailed interviews with departmental managers responsible for employees and their development, to a simple memo or questionnaire asking those concerned to outline their requirements for the year ahead in line with departmental objectives. The method chosen therefore, is left entirely to the departmental management involved in collecting the data and will obviously depend on the resources available. However an important source of information on individual needs will be the Employee Assessment and Development Scheme.

4. *Structuring the Training Plan*
To assist the person responsible for formulating the Training Plan an outline structure is attached. This model Training Plan is divided into six sections:

1. Strategic aims of the Department
2. Major operational issues facing the Department
3. Training and Development priorities
4. Departmental Personnel Summary
5. Training Budget
6. Training and Development Action Plan

This, it should be emphasised, is not the only format that is acceptable but represents good practice in basing employee development on the real needs of the Department as well as on each individual's natural desire for personal and career development.

Nevertheless, in determining whether a Department's training and development plan is acceptable the Director of Personnel will as a minimum standard require the information referred to in sections 4, 5 and 6 of the model plan. That is:

- the Departmental Personnel Summary
- the Departmental Training Budget (analysed as appropriate)
- the Training and Development Action Plan.

The Action Plan is intended to encompass only *off-the-job* training and development activities. The development of staff through work activities (special projects, job rotation, coaching by their Manager etc.) should be planned and managed through the Employee Assessment and Development Scheme.

[The model plan which follows has a cover sheet set out as follows]

GLASGOW CITY COUNCIL
MODEL PLAN

LIBRARIES DEPARTMENT
TRAINING AND DEVELOPMENT PLAN FOR 1991/92

Compiled by:
Name.........................
Designation.....................
Date............. ....

Approved by.....................
Date............................

POLICY STATEMENT
Departments with their own training policy statement should
incorporate it here.

INTRODUCTION – Council Policy Statement

The Director of Libraries recognises the Council's Policy for the
training and development of its staff which states:

"The Council recognises that training has an important contribution to make in the achievement of its corporate objectives and in
the maintenance of an effective, well motivated workforce.

The Council is therefore prepared to make available appropriate
training facilities which will enable employees to acquire the
aptitude, skills, knowledge and qualifications necessary to
perform effectively the duties and responsibilities of their posts.
The training provided will also take account of the needs of
employees to develop their potential for future employment at
more senior levels".

This plan sets out the Libraries Department's approach to the implementation of the Council's training and development policy objectives which are as follows:

1. to ensure that the Council has sufficient trained, qualified and experienced employees to meet its service needs and to ensure its continuing effectiveness in providing services;
2. to provide the training needed to enable employees to perform their present jobs more effectively and to acquire the necessary new skills when they move into new or different areas of work;
3. to assist employees to develop their potential and to realise their aspirations for career progression consistent with the needs of both the Council and individual employees;
4. to ensure that there is equality of opportunity for employees to obtain systematic training;
5. to meet the training and development needs of employees in the most effective way, in terms of quality and cost, by using the Council's own resources or, where this is not appropriate, by the utilisation of external training facilities and services.

The Plan is split into six sections:

1. Strategic Aims of the Department
2. Major operational issues facing the Department
3. Training and development priorities
4. Departmental Personnel Summary
5. Training Budget
6. Training and Development Action Plan (for off-the-job activities)

This document therefore constitutes the Libraries Department's record of intent regarding the training and development of its employees in line with the departmental objectives and plans for the year 1991/1992.

The Plan takes account of the training and development needs of all employees within the department arising from:

- council policies including commitments arising from the manifesto of the majority political group;
- current and future job requirements;

- the need to improve or maintain the performance of employees within their jobs;
- developing employees with potential;
- any special needs of groups or individual employees resulting from technological change, reorganisation or the introduction of new procedures within the department;
- needs arising from the Council's Employee Assessment and Development Scheme.

Responsibilities for the formulation and implementation of the plan are as shown overleaf.

Signed...........................

Director of......................

ANALYSIS OF TRAINING RESPONSIBILITY

ACTION	RESPONSIBILITY/ACCOUNTABILITY LEVEL
Formulation of Departmental Training and Development Policy and the approval of outline Training Plans and subsequent budgetted expenditure policy	Director/Depute Director level in association, where appropriate, with the Director of Personnel relative to overall Council
*	*
Identifying the training and development needs of employees within the department in accordance with departmental objectives/plans, to include the Council's Assessment & Development Scheme where appropriate	All management and first line Supervisors/Managers, who are responsible for supervising employees
*	*
Providing facilities/resources within the department for on-the-job training and development of employees where appropriate	All management and first line supervisors/managers, who are responsible for supervising employees
*	*

Arranging the release of employees for attendance at appropriate internal or external courses/seminars including further education	All management and first line supervisors/managers, who are responsible for supervising employees
*	*
Ensuring that the skills and knowledge gained by employees from training and development activities are applied and used in the performance of their job	All management and first line supervisors/managers, who are responsible for supervising employees
*	*
Providing data for the Departmental Training Plan from an analysis of training and development needs of the employees concerned, including recommendations, where appropriate, for the training sources/methods to be used in satisfying these needs	All management and first line supervisors/managers, who are responsible for supervising employees
*	*
Reviewing and evaluating the results of training and development in terms of the sources/methods used relative to their cost-effectiveness and required job performance of the employees concerned	All management and first line supervisors/managers, who are responsible for supervising employees in conjunction with the Departmental Training Co-ordinator
*	*
Sourcing and collecting the data for the Departmental Training Plan, to include formulating the Training Plan from information received	Departmental Training Co-ordinator
*	*

Provision of advice, assistance and guidance on training and development policy, methods, sources and activities, to include formulating the Departmental Training Plan and subsequent evaluation	Director of Personnel through central Training Co-ordinators in conjunction with the Departmental Training Co-ordinator

*

Training Administration Records to include attendance at internal and external courses and courses of further education at college etc.	Departmental Training Co-ordinator in conjunction with all management and first line supervisors/managers who are responsible for supervising employees

*

Provision of centrally organised internal courses for all Council employees on a wide range of subjects, in order to satisfy specific/common training and development needs as identified from Departmental Training Plans	Director of Personnel through central Training Co-ordinators

* * * * *

SECTION ONE
STRATEGIC AIMS OF THE DEPARTMENT
Training and development of staff is an important investment in supporting fulfilment of key departmental aims. The key aims of your department should be listed here.

They may be derived from such sources as the manifesto of the majority political group, from Council and Committee decisions, from internal strategy documents or from the annual budget process.

LIST KEY AIMS:
Glasgow City Libraries as a Department of Glasgow City Council has three strategic aims:

1. in lending services to provide library material in all forms for home use by the public, community information and enquiry services from a network of libraries;

2. in reference services to maintain by acquisition and presentation a comprehensive collection of books and other material for reference and study; provide from that material and through computer databases a wide ranging reference and public information service; and
3. in administrative services to control and manage the department and provide support services for all departments.

SECTION TWO
MAJOR OPERATIONAL ISSUES

At a more detailed level training and development needs for groups of staff and individuals can arise from policy and procedural changes, new legislation, new technology, new working methods as a result of the demands of competitive tendering or a range of other specific factors. The implications of such changes may be reflected in the outcomes of Employee Assessment and Development interviews.

This section should focus only on the main issues seen as having important training and development implications for the department.

LIST MAIN ISSUES:

1. The implementation of changes in work practice arising from the MSU report on lending and reference services.
2. Extend the use of the automated issue system to include fines for overdue material and variable loan periods.
3. Continue with the introduction of CD-ROMs to replace or augment hard copy.
4. Increase the use of libraries by 5%.
5. Reduce departmental absenteeism.

SECTION THREE
TRAINING AND DEVELOPMENT PRIORITIES

Having outlined the main challenges facing the Department in the previous two sections, this section should be used to highlight the main skills, knowledge and attitudes that will have to be acquired by employees as a result. What training needs are implied in the strategy and in the operational issues? What has emerged from Employee Assessment and Development? Another source of information on training needs will be the person specification drawn up prior to recruiting new members of staff. Where possible, reference should be made to the main employee groupings for whom a particular training and development response is appropriate.

LIST TRAINING & DEVELOPMENT PRIORITIES:

1. As a result of the Management Services review, four new posts of Heads of Division have been created. These posts carry considerably greater responsibility for budget allocation and the monitoring and control of expenditure within a division of approximately ten service points. The new postholders will almost certainly require training in budgeting and financial control, the departmental budgeting system and in adapting to change.

2. Manual workers will be included in a greater variety of courses in the coming years. It is this department's intention to train all manual workers in Customer Care and Sensory Awareness. We also intend to introduce an updated general safety course as well as a Supervisory Skills programme for Shift Leaders. Drivers will undergo HGV training in order to comply with EEC regulations.

3. Training in Employee Assessment and Development will continue to include grades AP2 down to GS1. All employees will attend the two-day in-house course.

4. Induction training (half-day) for all new entrants will take place within the first month of commencing employment and library assistants will receive additional training.

5. All Mitchell Library Staff will attend a new course, "Sensory Awareness", to enable them to cope better with customers with sensory disabilities. Customer Care for library assistants will be introduced this year (especially for new entrants).

6. The Young Peoples Services Department will continue to offer a variety of courses to enable staff to either update or acquire new skills in order that the service can be maintained and improved. For example, courses in Storytelling, Book Selection, School Visits and Merchandising and Display.

7. Discipline, Grievance and Counselling – it is intended that all designated supervisors attend this course to enable them to deal with changes in the Council's Absence Monitoring Scheme as well as enhancing their managerial skills.

8. The First Line – the supervisory development programme will be run in-house for the first time this year and focus on the particular needs of the department's supervisors.

9. The need for training in Marketing the Service has been highlighted by the EAD Scheme and priority will be placed on seeking appropriate courses to meet individual and departmental needs.

SECTION FOUR
DEPARTMENTAL PERSONNEL SUMMARY
This section should set out the actual establishment levels for the main categories of staff in the Department. The way staff are classified may vary slightly from department to department but a common classification might be: Management, Supervisory, Technical, Professional, Administrative/Clerical, Manual. Please be specific in defining each group.

GROUP & SECTION	NUMBER
APT & C	
Directorate	4
Administrative services	44
Lending services	351
Reference services	101
Total APT & C	500
MANUAL	
Administrative services	44
Lending services	73
Total manual	117
TEMPORARY	10
MATERNITY LEAVE	16

SECTION FIVE
DEPARTMENTAL TRAINING BUDGET 1990–1991
Total Training Budget   £-----(insert figure)
NB. Please include estimated expenditure on conferences.

DEPARTMENTAL TRAINING BUDGET ANALYSIS
If appropriate please indicate below the main sub-headings within your department's Training Budget (e.g. Further Education, Courses, Continuing Professional Development etc.)

LIST MAIN BUDGET SUB-HEADINGS:

SECTION SIX

THE TRAINING AND DEVELOPMENT ACTION PLAN

On the following pages you should list the off-the-job activities planned to meet the Training and Development priorities identified in Section Three. Account should also be taken of agreed individual training and development activities identified through the Employee Assessment and Development Scheme.

It may be useful to use separate sheets for the various categories of staff identified in Section Four. Some Departments may also wish to separate Further Education provision from other development activities.

DRAWING UP THE ACTION PLAN

Use an A4 sheet of paper (landscape) to draw up your departmental action plan. Head each sheet with the name of the Department and the Staff Group. Please use a separate sheet for each staff group listed in Section Four. Each sheet should be divided into vertical columns with the following headings:

1. Employee Group or Individual
2. Off-the-Job Training and Development Activity/Course Title
3. Objectives of the Activity
4. Responsibility
5. Duration (in days)
6. No. of Employees involved
7. Budget (where appropriate) in £

Each column should be completed as follows:

COLUMN 1 – should identify as specifically as possible the groups and individuals for whom a particular training and development activity is intended.

COLUMN 2 – should specify the nature of the activity. This should include the full range of possible off-the-job training and development opportunities including:

Secondments	Open Learning
Seminars	Further Education
Visits	User Groups
Conferences	

It should also wherever possible include details of the supplier of any training or other service (e.g. Central Personnel Training and Development, College, external trainer etc.).

COLUMN 3 – should specify as precisely as possible why the training and development activity is being carried out and what it is hoped to achieve. It should be possible after training and development has occurred to say whether the objectives have been achieved.

COLUMN 4 – should name the member of staff who will have responsibility for organising each training and development activity and for ensuring it is carried out.

COLUMN 5 – provides information on the duration in days of each activity. This will in most cases be best expressed as the number of days away from normal duties (e.g. a one year course of further education will probably involve 30 days away from normal duties if on a day release basis).

COLUMN 6 – provides information on the number of employees involved.

COLUMN 7 – provides an estimate of the cost of the activity where this is appropriate. This should take into account travel, subsistence and other reimbursements, as well as normal course fees.

As the above case study illustrates, training should not be viewed as something which takes place in isolation from the employing organization, although some of the activities may take place outside that organization. In establishing the training needs of the individual, the manager is also required to be able to justify them in terms of the organization's needs. Extracts from Glasgow's Employee Assessment and Development Scheme Handbook are reproduced in Chapter 10.

CHAPTER NINE

Planning training and development: first considerations

It is the manager's responsibility to help staff to realize their full potential, improving their performance through making the most of their abilities. In many cases the manager may be the person conducting the training, and even if that is not the case, they will almost certainly be evaluating its outcome in day-to-day performance, not only in the period immediately following the training but continuously. Being a manager also implies taking on a much wider role within the organization as a whole, for example as a member of a planning committee. That wider role will help considerably in the management of the training activity for the LIS. First there will be a range of useful points of reference throughout the organization in the form of other managers who, although running departments with a different specialist focus, are likely to share common areas of responsibility such as staff training and development. There may well be regular managers' meetings, which will act as a focus for such discussion, as well as providing the opportunity to get to know each other and the work of the various departments in much more detail. A second point of reference will be any central department which may exist to serve training needs across the organization. This may be part of the personnel function, which in the absence of a separate training function will also be able to provide useful advice. The personnel department is the one you will be most likely to consult about training policies, training contracts, and any statements about training which may be included in the written conditions of employment sent out to new recruits. These will have set the expectations of new staff as to what will actually happen from their first day of employment.

Having already received answers to the initial questions about organizational guidelines on training, you will now be aware of a number of factors which will have to be taken into account when designing a departmental training programme. Perhaps it would be helpful at this stage to draw up a more detailed management checklist, looking first at in-house policies and facilities by establishing answers to the following questions:

- Is there a central training department?
- Does any single person have overall responsibility for training throughout the organization, and if so, who?
- Is there a central training policy?
- Are policies and procedures set out in any sort of staff manual?
- Is there a central training budget?
- Who controls training expenditure?
- Do departments have separate/supplementary training budgets?
- What sort of in-house courses are available?
- What specialist knowledge can be called on?
- What training skills exist?
- What training facilities and equipment are there?

The answers to such questions should help you to assess whether the existing in-house training facilities and programmes would be relevant, or could be adapted to suit your requirements.

The organizational climate, especially senior management support for, and encouragement of, training and development, will have a strong influence on its successful implementation. The research referred to in Chapter 7 indicates the increasing importance of training as perceived by employing organizations, with a number of them setting up central training departments and appointing those responsible for them at a senior, often director, level, and offering increased training opportunities for staff at all levels. A positive organizational climate is also likely to be supportive of the use of appropriate external training. However, as with all expenditure, both of money and of time, it is always up to the individual manager to make the case for it in terms of organizational benefits.

When planning training for a specific department it is important to adopt a coordinated approach, designing an overall training plan which will take into account the present needs of, and future plans for the service (as perceived in relation to the future needs of the organization), while retaining the flexibility essential to be able to meet the often very different needs of each member of staff who may be undergoing training at any one time.

It is essential that all training is carefully planned, from the identification of needs and the ways in which these might be satisfied, to the incorporation of training costs into the budget. Timing is also crucial; first, the individual will need certain training before he or she can progress to the next stage, and secondly the period of time between training sessions needs to be long enough for earlier training to be assimilated and put into practice, but not so long that earlier learning is lost and unable to be built on without further repetition. Training may be task-specific or broader-based, such as that aimed at developing administrative and organizational skills, or relating to the communication and interpersonal aspects of the job. The whole process needs to be structured into a logical sequence for maximum benefit.

With some activities it may be appropriate for several members of staff to undertake training together, as in the case where new procedures or new services are being introduced, such as automated cataloguing, additional online services or a help desk. It is also important to remember that you as manager have to sell the idea of the training, not only to senior management but also to those who are to receive it. They need to be assured that this is a beneficial activity, not a threatening one, and that it is being planned to suit their specific needs. No matter how much training is provided, if the reasons for it are not explained sensitively and in positive terms the training itself is not likely to achieve maximum impact.

It is good practice to involve the individual in the total process – in assessing their own needs, in setting objectives, in talking through alternative training methods as to their appropriateness, and after the event, by encouraging feedback and discussion on each piece of training, not just with you as the manager, but also with other members of the department. This can lead to an enhanced teamwork approach, with the sharing of experience having valuable spin-off in terms of staff relationships and LIS operations and initiatives. The full value of training is then much more likely to be perceived and the individual more highly motivated to pursue it with enthusiasm and to invest the necessary personal effort. The achievement of training objectives may lead to expectations of rewards, such as promotion, or perhaps a salary increase. It is important that any training programme is therefore developed within the framework of an overall career structure, so that any expectations are clearly based on fact rather than surmise. This is clearly demonstrated in the CSIRO case study in Chapter 12.

Some employers, for example, currently offer a bonus on the achievement of Associate or other equivalent professional status. Additional responsibility may not always be regarded strictly as a reward, although most staff would see it as a mark of confidence in their ability and an enhancement of their status, and it could naturally follow the successful outcome of training. This also needs to be built into the initial discussion in planning the training programme, so that in addition to meeting the specific objectives of each training event, the individual will be able to establish other longer-term goals.

The planning of your departmental training may well start with a review of the service and an examination of any staff manual or overall training policy to see what is generally regarded as being essential for all staff. You could then focus on any specialist training provided to other functions or departments. It would be wise before going further to have an open discussion with the training or personnel department about such aspects as, for example, payment of course fees, study leave, day release, and the provision of training materials. This will also provide you with the opportunity to put forward or clarify matters relating specifically to LIS training and development, for example employer support for initial and continuing professional education, opportunities for the pursuit of paraprofessional qualifications such as the City and Guilds examinations, and what such support might consist of in terms of, say, the provision of study time or the payment of fees. There may also be other general questions that you wish to raise.

Evaluation and monitoring

It would be helpful at this stage to establish whether there are any centrally designed feedback mechanisms currently in use to evaluate training and development, such as questionnaires or checklists, and to obtain samples of these so that you can feed these requirements into your planning, and also to consider whether such forms need to be adapted for departmental use. They may in fact form part of the organization's appraisal system, and as such be the standard means of evaluation and feedback.

Training and development activities are pursued in order that certain objectives can be met. In planning these you will need to think about their evaluation in terms of their effectiveness in achieving those objectives. This is well illustrated by the Glasgow and CSIRO case studies in Chapters, 8, 10 and 12.

Evaluation can take place in several ways, as follows:

- Participant response via completion of a post-event questionnaire, or a written report or short presentation to other staff about what the event achieved.
- Regular consultation between the manager and the person under-going the training or development programme.
- Ongoing monitoring of individual performance by the manager through observation or by performance tests which require demonstration of the successful application of the skill or knowledge acquired. Rather than being regarded as a formal academic exercise these can be incorporated into daily work activities, with the trainee being asked to handle live problems under supervision and with subsequent feedback.

Evaluation and monitoring activities can add another dimension to team-building, but need to be presented in a positive way to staff and handled sensitively. They also need to be well structured so that they provide the information you are seeking and contribute to the ongoing appraisal process. Where problems are identified, prompt management follow-up will be required while the problem is still fresh in the mind of the trainee, otherwise the benefits of other parts of the training may be lost. Swift management action is also important as a sign of the manager's continued interest and overall confidence in the individual concerned.

Some organizations may also require an evaluation of training and development as part of their regular review of recruitment policy, looking to see if there are links between staff turnover and the availability and effectiveness of a staff development programme.

The training budget

The personnel or training department may well control a central training budget, which is something else that could influence your own training activities. In the research study *Best practice* [1] approximately

half of the participating organizations exercised central control of training budgets, whereas the other half operated departmental training
budgets. Another interesting fact which emerged was that even where
there were central budgets, these were often viewed as being for
general training, e.g. management and business skills required across
the organization, with a supplementary budget controlled by departments and intended purely for their specialist needs. The availability of
in-house training will influence the planning of your budget, but this
should not be the sole factor in determining whether to take up internal
opportunities for training or to seek those on offer externally.

It must be remembered that even in-house courses cost money: both
the person running the course and those attending it are not available to
carry out other work for the period of time during which the training
takes place. In some cases an outside lecturer or agency is brought in to
design and conduct courses, often charging quite a high fee for doing
so. However, the enlightened organization sees such costs as an investment in its own future development, and may also regard them as
central and not attributable to particular departments.

On-the-job training also has a cost in terms of staff time – not just the
time spent giving the training, but also that required for its preparation.
Staff time costs vary not only according to the grade on which each
person is paid, but also according to their specific abilities, which may
dictate that in some circumstances only one person would be able to
carry out a particular task. If that service is required regularly, for
example translation, or some other specialist service for which that
person's specialist skills are required, it would not be cost-effective for
them to be seconded to the training role too frequently. In the case of
online training the costs of using each database also need to be taken
into consideration, although there are ways of minimizing these. For
example, the use of 'live' enquiries in the training process, with the
trainee in the passenger seat at first. Also take advantage of the free
online time and free or low-priced seminars offered by many database
providers and hosts – these can make a useful contribution to the training budget.

Even where there is a central training budget it may still be the case
that training specific to your department will be under your control, and
shown as just one cost centre within your overall budget. However, you
may still find it helpful to breakdown the expenditure, for example by
person and/or type of training. This could prove useful in staff

planning, recruitment and service development. It might also assist in broader organizational planning. Budgeting for training is part of your overall financial planning but it should be regarded not only as part of the cost of running the library or information service; it also needs to be balanced against the organizational and departmental benefits which accrue from staff development and training.

Angela Bridgeland [2] suggests that, in addition to the direct costs of training, e.g. trainers fees, materials, equipment and administrative costs, managers also have to consider the hidden costs. Among these she notes cost benefits, that is, what would the cost of *not* doing the training be against the direct cost, and, what would be done better as a result of training?

BACIE, the British Association for Commercial and Industrial Education, runs a series of workshops and seminars called Training for Profit. BACIE suggests that this approach will help training managers to use the techniques of financial analysis in order to:

- Relate training to the objectives and competitive strategy of the organization
- Develop training to improve the levels of profitability and financial performance
- Balance training investment between meeting long-term and short-term needs.

Librarians and information managers could well find this approach, which is also described by Darling [3], useful in helping them to argue the case for training investment, as well as assisting them in the design and implementation of training.

References

1. Webb, S. P. (1991) *Best practice?: continuing professional development for library/ information staff in UK professional firms*. British Library R & D Report 6039. Berkhamsted: Sylvia P. Webb.
2. Bridgeland, A. (1990) Evaluation aspects of staff development. In *Library staff development: proceedings of the first national seminar, July 1990*, ed. I. Hiscock. Adelaide: South Australian College of Advanced Education.
3. Darling, P. (1990) *Training for profit: developing a high performance workforce*. London: BACIE.

CHAPTER TEN

Identifying training and development needs

Planning any programme of training and development needs careful thought and must be based on identified needs. If there has been no previous training policy for LIS staff, then a good way of starting would be to have a departmental meeting. If you offer your library service throughout the day, as favoured by most organizations, then you may need to ask your staff if they would be prepared to stay on after work for such a discussion. Another possibility is to run the meeting twice for half the staff at a time – this could be particularly appropriate where job sharing or other forms of part-time or shift work operate. This format will require detailed recording and feedback from the manager, who will also need to coordinate the main outcomes of each meeting.

The same open form of exchange could be equally useful even when there is an existing departmental policy, for example for the newly appointed manager it presents an opportunity to interact with staff outside the department without the usual operational constraints. It allows the manager to see the staff as a team and to observe relationships and assess possible similarities and differences in training needs. It provides a forum within which to exchange information about future potential developments within the organization, and their subsequent impact on the department. Such meetings need to be carefully handled if they are to allow people to contribute freely, while ensuring that all essential items are covered in the time allocated; skilled structuring and control of the meeting is vital.

The outcome of this meeting or meetings should be summarized as a series of main points and circulated to all LIS staff to help them consider their own individual training needs, and perhaps in clarifying where and how their roles fit into the team, the department and the organization. It is also a good idea to send a copy either to the Director of Personnel and Training or to any senior executive who may have ultimate responsibility for LIS matters. This will (a) inform them, underlining the importance of LIS training and development in an organizational context, and (b) demonstrate your own commitment as a manager to training and development. The next stage would be a series of meetings between individuals and the manager, in which the process of identifying individual needs would take place. The list of points developed from the initial meeting should serve as a useful starting point for these sessions, avoiding the need for a ground-clearing exercise and putting the discussion into a sharper focus.

The role of appraisal and assessment

Identification of training needs usually forms part of the appraisal process where, following discussion of the individual's achievements, level of job satisfaction and areas of concern, the individual and the manager will jointly discuss the ways in which the latter may be resolved. This is likely to include the identification of certain training needs. Of course, not all areas of concern will be resolved by training alone: they could equally require a counselling element or one of the many other means of individual development, examples of which are listed in Section 5 of the second Glasgow case study, which follows. It should also be remembered that not all problems are brought about by the actions of the trainee; they could just as easily be attributable to organizational policies or procedures.

The appraisal, described in Part One as an essential element of good overall personnel practice, is an important factor in the training and development process. The identification of training needs may take place within a single appraisal interview, or may be a follow-up to the main interview. Whichever way you choose to organize this, meetings between individual members of staff and the manager need to be arranged in advance, written into the diary, and treated with the importance they deserve. It is essential that the manager and the member of staff have a short discussion at the time of arranging the date, about the purpose of the forthcoming meeting and what each needs to think about in advance. A questionnaire or checklist might help in the preparation. It is quite common practice to use a standard 'self-appraisal' form which can help structure the thoughts of the individual and provide a basis for discussion. These could be modified to suit departmental needs and have a supplementary checklist specifically designed to act as a training action plan, of which both the individual concerned and the manager will keep a copy. Most standard appraisal forms have a section relating to training and development needs.

The training and development plan shown in the first Glasgow City Libraries case study (Chapter 8) makes regular reference to the related Employee Assessment and Development Scheme. This is a scheme which operates in all departments of the City of Glasgow's local authority. To ensure that the scheme operates efficiently and that staff receive consistency of approach, a handbook is provided to guide supervisors and managers in how to carry out their assessment and development responsibilities. Extracts from the handbook form the next case study.

Case study: Glasgow City Libraries II

CITY OF GLASGOW

EMPLOYEE ASSESSMENT AND DEVELOPMENT SCHEME HANDBOOK

1. STATEMENT OF INTENT
Every employee of Glasgow District Council must, as a condition of their employment, undertake a personal assessment and development interview with their immediate supervisor at least once a year. The Council fully recognizes that its efficiency and effectiveness is dependent upon a high standard of employee performance. Accordingly, the assessment and development of employees will be a priority throughout all departments of the Council.

The scheme aims to ensure that:

(a) employees clearly understand what is expected of them in their job and have an opportunity to agree key tasks and performance standards with their managers;
(b) the performance of employees in their jobs is reviewed regularly on a joint basis between managers and subordinates;
(c) employees' development activities fully reflect the Council's wider corporate policies and objectives;

(d) employees receive the training and development they need to improve their current job performance and to prepare them for their future careers;

(e) employees whose performance continues to be unsatisfactory will be given assistance by means of counselling.

The Council agrees that the process of assessment will not be used to initiate disciplinary action which should be handled under separate procedures. The scheme is not linked to pay.

2. PURPOSE
The main purpose of the scheme is to ensure high standards of employee performance by means of:

(a) setting clear tasks and standards of performance;
(b) regularly reviewing progress towards them;
(c) identifying and meeting training and development needs;
(d) improving communication;
(e) increasing motivation through regular feedback.

3. THE ASSESSMENT AND DEVELOPMENT FORM
Before going on to explain the assessment and development process in detail it is necessary to provide a brief decription of the assessment and development form. It is intended that Employee Assessment and Development should operate as a joint process between postholders and reporting officers. Each should therefore have an opportunity to set out their views about the information required by the form prior to the assessment and development interview at which the final version of the form will be agreed.

The form has five main sections:

Section 1 – Task and target review
The key areas of responsibility agreed at the previous year's assessment interview are listed in order of priority. This involves taking the items listed at Section 3 on the form for the previous year and transferring them to Section 1 of the new assessment form. It is accepted that external pressures and constraints or changes in priorities may affect the achievement of these tasks. They may therefore be an amended list compared to that originally set.

Section 2 – Performance
In this section postholder and reporting officer review the previous year's performance in relation to the tasks and targets set. It is important that both parties are as explicit as possible about the level of performance achieved. Performance above the standard set should be specifically highlighted and the reasons for this discussed as should any areas of performance below the standard set.

Section 3 – Tasks and targets for the coming year
It is important that this part of the form is completed well, for the success of the scheme will depend on clear, realistic and assessable tasks being set.

The intention is that the postholder and reporting officer should discuss and agree the tasks and targets for the coming year and put these as far as possible in order of priority. This is not intended to be a full job description but to highlight those key tasks that are essential to the performance of an individual's job. They should provide a clear under-standing of the postholder's responsibilities. Most will be tasks that continue from year to year and which are necessary to maintain the service being provided. A minority may be new tasks reflecting the need to develop a new emphasis within the job.

Tasks should be written so that they not only describe the activities being carried out but also the desired outcomes arising from them. The outcomes must, however be within the control of the postholder.

A task should, if possible, consist of a single sentence constructed around three elements: a verb, an object of action and a result. They should be realistic, as specific as possible, readily understandable and imply a means of measurement. Some examples are provided at the end of this note.

Targets should be established for each task. There may be more than one target per task. Targets may be related to quantity or quality. Targets should be measurable wherever possible. Typical measures might be completion dates, production levels, rates of return, activity levels, defect levels, complaints, backlog, response time or meeting financial targets.

Not all tasks can be measured objectively. In some cases a judgement may have to be made regarding the performance level achieved. In such cases the reasons for a particular judgement being made should be openly and fully discussed between postholder and reporting officer at the assessment interview.

The tasks and targets of postholders and reporting officers must be properly related to each other. A single task of a superior may give rise to several distinct tasks among subordinates. Care should be taken that tasks for the same result are not carried elsewhere in the organisation.

Managers of staff within the assessment and development scheme should always have as one of their key tasks the completion of assessment interviews and implementation of agreed development activities.

Section 4 – Future development needs

This section should take account not only of the training and development needs highlighted by performance in the previous year but also any such needs arising from the tasks and targets set for the coming year. Reference should be made to the checklist below Section 4 on the assessment form. It directs attention to some of the main attributes and skills that are likely to have relevance to job performance. [These have been listed below as the form has not been reproduced]

job knowledge	technical competence
developing subordinates	planning & organisation
motivating others	coping with change
quality management	sensitivity/tact
communication skills	decision-making
assertiveness	leadership
service to customers	delegation
personal relationships	financial awareness
marketing	

Postholder and reporting officer should try to agree what skills and attributes are of particular relevance to the job under discussion.

There may be some aspects of performance that can be improved by other management action in support of the postholder (e.g. the provision of additional equipment or finance) and this can be discussed and recorded at this stage.

Section 5 – Development plan
In this section details of the actions to be taken to develop the post-holder during the coming year should be set out. It should be remembered that there is a wide variety of ways of meeting the training and development needs of staff. Reference should be made to the checklist below Section 5 of the assessment form which highlights some of the main ways in which employees can be trained and developed. [As the form has not been reproduced the checklist is given here.]

work experience	presentations	reading
seminars	working parties	coaching
secondments	open learning	courses/conferences
projects	job swaps	visits
user groups	further education	private study

Training should take place when learning on the job is either impossible or likely to be too slow or ineffective. Training will improve job performance if it meets a real job-related need. This section of the assessment form is also the place to plan further education provision if this is seen as relevant.

Having worked through the form during the interview a definitive version is completed and signed by both the postholder and the reporting officer. If agreement is not possible this must be recorded at the relevant points on the form.

4. THE ASSESSMENT AND DEVELOPMENT PROCESS
The assessment and development process will normally be completed within the period 1 February to 30 April each year unless other arrangements are agreed with the Director of Personnel.

Each department will produce a timetable for implementation before 1 February each year.

Stage 1 – Independent Analysis and Assessment
The first stage comprises the following steps:

(a) The postholder (the member of staff concerned) independently makes a self assessment using the self-assessment form to prompt ideas. This involves looking back to Section 3 of the form for the previous year and transferring the agreed tasks and targets to Section 1 of the new form (if there has been no previous assessment proceed immediately to Section 3). The postholder then prepares his or her views on whether the tasks and targets have been achieved (Section 2). Next comes a preliminary view by the postholder about the key tasks and targets for the coming year (Section 3) followed by a review of their own development needs (Section 4).

(b) The reporting officer (the immediate supervisor) at the same time undertakes a similar independent assessment prior to the assessment interview.

(c) The postholder and the reporting officer exchange forms for each to consider the other's assessment prior to the assessment interview.

Stage 2 – Joint analysis and assessment
Having made their own analysis and assessment the postholder and reporting officer meet together to openly discuss their views on past performance, agree tasks and targets for the coming year and identify training and development needs. This involves completion of the assessment form which should be signed by postholder and reporting officer. It should be remembered that effective interviews will require both participants to:

PREPARE

CONCENTRATE ON PERFORMANCE NOT PERSONALITY

AGREE OBJECTIVES

An effective interview will also require the reporting officer to:

LISTEN AND ASK QUESTIONS

Assessment and development interviews should be conducted in private and away from interruptions.

Stage 3 – Review by the reporting officer's supervisor
At the conclusion of the assessment interview postholder and reporting officer should take copies of the agreed and signed form and forward the original to the countersigning officer.

The role of the countersigning officer is to:

(a) confirm that the agreed tasks and targets are appropriate;

(b) ensure fairness and consistency in the application of the assessment process;

(c) resolve any outstanding areas of disagreement.

In the event of a postholder feeling aggrieved after completion of this process he or she may appeal to the head of Department. In the unlikely event of no agreement being possible at that stage the postholder may invoke the Council's grievance procedure.

Countersigned forms should normally be returned to the postholder and reporting officer within two weeks.

Stage 4 – Retention of forms
As with all personnel records the assessment form is confidential. The postholder retains a copy of the form. A copy of the Development Plan portion of the form (Section 5) should be forwarded to the member of staff responsible for the Departmental Training Plan so that it may be taken account of there.

Assessment and development forms will not be used by reporting officers or countersigning officers as references in respect of job applications by employees.

5. MANAGING THE SCHEME
An Assessment and Development Scheme is not something that can be installed and left to run itself. People's skills in running the scheme will improve over time and the benefits will increase correspondingly. In addition managers will need to monitor the operation of the scheme and improve and develop it when necessary. For that reason each department of the Council should review its experience of the scheme annually.

[The handbook continues with a note about the importance of effective communication in the assessment and development process. This has been incorporated in the following summary.]

The annual review should, in communication terms:

- *summarise* all major points embraced by formal discussion
- *allow* thorough examination of the situation from both points of view
- *allow* jobholders to understand their manager's view of how they have performed and what is expected of them
- *help* to discuss and define needs for development, training and experience.

Its success therefore hinges on the principles of:

Objectivity on the part of the assessor and the jobholder.
Two-way communication and all that this involves.
Discussions which are treated in confidence by both parties.
Agreement by both parties on subsequent follow-up action.

[The note continues with some hints on the use of non-verbal behaviour, stressing the importance of listening and of minimising distractions. It then continues with examples of good spoken communication techniques to achieve desired results, e.g. the use of open-ended questions, probing, encouraging. The importance of conveying understanding is also emphasised. Guidance is also given on the selection of appropriate and specific verbs with examples of those found most helpful in describing key tasks. These are then set into context with further examples, two of which are reproduced below.]

Format of sentence:

VERB . . . . SUBJECT OF ACTION . . . . DESIRED RESULT

e.g. Provide . . . training courses . . . to ensure the competence of first time managers.

Assess . . . trainee work performance . . . to identify the extent of further training needs.

[This section of the handbook concludes with a useful summary of the basic rules of assessment interviewing as set out below]

INTERVIEWING SKILLS	BASIC RULES
1 BE PREPARED	Be familiar with postholder's past history
	Study relevant documents
	Appropriate seating arrangements
	No disturbance
2 ESTABLISH THE RIGHT ATMOSPHERE	Ice breaker/conversation unrelated to interview
	Outline objectives & structure of interview
	Emphasise this is a joint discussion

3 FOLLOW A PATTERN	Listen & provide feedback Use structure of form to guide discussion Investigate specific examples Assist postholder to identify problem areas Give recognition for a job well done
4 ENCOURAGE FRANK DISCUSSION	Reporting officer always controls situation Discuss results, targets, difficulties, aspirations Adopt constructive approach, ask open questions Identify training & development needs Obtain commitment to agreed tasks & targets Both participants to be fully objective
5 DECIDE ACTION	Motivate postholder to perform to best ability Postholder to be clear on action required Form to be agreed & signed by both parties

The above case study illustrates the information necessary to build up a complete picture from which training and development needs can be identified.

As has already been said, the necessary training identified may be task-oriented or person-oriented; it could be on-the-job, self-study or course-based. The methods and techniques, which are described in more detail in a later chapter, need to be carefully chosen with the individual in mind. People respond in different ways to the presentation of information: some learn better by seeing, others by listening; some from reading or working on their own, others in a group setting with an appropriate expert on call to answer questions. This is something which is not always easy to assess until you know a person reasonably well and are able to judge more accurately those approaches likely to result in a positive outcome. Even then, extraneous factors may well influence a person's response to training at any point in time.

It is good practice to involve other members of the team in the training process, allowing them to pass on their own specialist expertise: for example, if one member of staff exhibits particularly good telephone skills, they could be encouraged to develop a short training session on telephone techniques, and to carry out training on that topic for the department. This would in turn give them a sense of responsibility and achievement and a feeling of making a valuable contribution to the department and the organization. However, this must be done in a structured way with careful selection of the areas and individuals appropriate to such a method, otherwise bad habits as well as good can be passed on.

Having identified individual needs, your next step as manager is to see how these can best be implemented as part of an overall plan for the department. Some areas may well be best covered in-house, either within the department or through training available centrally within the organization. By setting up a programme where each person knows that, as they attain a certain stage, they will be attending a particular in-house course, considerable benefits are likely to occur both in terms of bringing about cohesiveness within the department and allowing the individuals concerned to make wider contacts throughout the organization. The spin-off in terms of increasing awareness about the LIS and what it can do should also not be overlooked.

If you are considering the use of external courses how do you set about identifying them and, even more important, evaluating them? Most professional associations organize a variety of training activities, as well as maintaining directories and databases of courses available from other agencies. Special-interest groups, either affiliated to the professional bodies or operating independently, also arrange conferences, seminars and other events relevant to the training process. There has been an increased emphasis over recent years on cooperative training across both the public and the private sectors, which could usefully be worked into your departmental training plan. This is discussed further in Chapter 14.

There are advantages and disadvantages to be considered regarding both in-house and externally generated training. For example, the benefits to an individual of being able to step back from the organization and consider matters objectively, to speak freely without organizational constraints, and above all to exchange ideas with and learn from those in other organizations, are considerable. On the other hand in-house training, if at the right level and having the appropriate focus, brings other benefits such as meeting those from other departments with whom there may have been little previous contact, the feeling of organizational 'belonging' and, particularly where the trainer is a member of staff, the opportunity for quick and direct follow-up as required.

You need to be aware of the range of training methods on offer to be able to draw up the most effective and coordinated programme. These are discussed further in Chapters 13 and 14.

CHAPTER ELEVEN

Designing the training programme

When designing a training programme, whether of a short or a longer-term duration, the key feature is the statement of objectives. Look at almost any commercial training directory and you will find for each course a note of its main aims and objectives, so that you as a purchaser of any of the courses will have a clear idea of what you can expect to be the outcomes of each course. This applies whether the course is a one-off standalone event or part of a series. There should also be an indication of the intended level of the course, and an indication of the training methods to be employed. The same practice of indicating key features applies when drawing up an in-house programme, which is likely to be a coordination of a number of different events or activities. Start with what you hope will be achieved. This will be as important for the person undergoing the training as for you as their manager. Trainees will be clear about what they should be working towards, and you will have a set of criteria against which to measure the success of the training. At Stoy Hayward, a leading UK accountancy practice, a programme was drawn up to meet the Library Association's registration requirements, which enables candidates to pursue chartered status. This was to take place over a period of 1 year, at the end of which the candidates would be able to assess their own professional development and seek Associate status of the Library Association. This programme with its objectives and methods can be seen in full in *Personal development in information work* [1]. However, the important thing about it was that it was also able to be adapted for use by those members of the department who were not pursuing a professional qualification but had demonstrated ability to work in a professional way, exhibiting good information skills along with other abilities and longer-term potential. This approach of developing a comprehensive programme has been found to be successful in other organizations, of which examples have been reproduced in *Best practice* [2], a study of continuing professional development for LIS staff in UK professional firms. Objectives should be stated clearly and concisely: it is not necessary to make a lengthy list to cover what is needed. Programmes can be designed to be applicable to all levels of LIS staff, incorporating internal and external elements and showing the points in time at which each module should be pursued and by which category of staff. This comprehensive approach has a hidden benefit, in that staff have a sense of organizational as well as departmental identity, sharing common goals through working on the same programme, even if they are pursuing different elements of it.

Training methods other than on-the-job will be discussed later, but what do you hope your staff will achieve in the longer term by following a training programme? What will form the detail underpinning the stated objectives? If we take those set out in the Stoy Hayward programme referred to earlier, they can be summarized as follows:

1. To ensure that the candidate receives a comprehensive induction to the library and information service, and to the organization as a whole
2. To explain the practical use of various professional skills and to ensure that the trainee is able to experience the use of these over a wide range of activities
3. To create an awareness of, and involve the candidate in, a range of management and supervisory activities
4. To develop a range of technical skills
5. To familiarize the candidate with training responsibilities
6. To develop the trainee's awareness of, and skills in, interpersonal relationships and communication.

As you can see from the above, the overall aim is to produce a high level of professional awareness and competence based on a broad understanding, as well as the effective and efficient use of skills. Although the Stoy Hayward scheme was designed initially to meet the registration requirements of the Library Association, the objectives are equally appropriate for members of staff not pursuing that particular route. But what should be covered in order to achieve this set of objectives? The induction process, described in Chapter 13, aims among other things to enable the trainee to see the direct relationship of the library/information service to its parent organization's objectives and activities. In order to achieve this, library and information staff will need to be able to make full use of their professional skills, including critical ability as referred to in the second objective listed above – already it is apparent that activities that will be developed to achieve one objective are also likely to assist in the achievement of others. The candidate may already have a knowledge of professional skills, perhaps gained from formal education, but with little opportunity to date to pursue the practical application of those skills – or alternatively, from experience not supported by the exposure to the underlying theory. Either way the knowledge may be limited to certain areas, so the need is to ensure that the candidate is not only aware of the range of skills which they could be using, but also of how to use them to maximum effect. Under the second objective the Stoy Hayward programme lists skills relating to:

- Enquiry work
- Scanning, abstracting and indexing
- .Classification and cataloguing
- Appreciation and use of non-book printed material such as looseleaf works, updating services, and the development of subject files
- Appreciation and use of online services
- Selection, acquisition and review of stock
- Inter-library loans
- Bibliographical work
- Library organization
- Promotion of the service
- Research
- Ongoing professional awareness of new services and events
- Specialized subject work in areas relevant to the organization's activities.

As you can see, a number of these will also support part of the aim of the induction process. Other objectives are similarly interrelated, for example (3), (5) and (6), with their common emphasis on styles of behaviour, especially the development of interpersonal and communication skills. These selected examples indicate the benefits of developing a training programme as a total package – the initial effort on the manager's part certainly results in a much more logical and better structured programme than could be achieved by a more ad hoc approach, and is more likely to result in a successful outcome both for the person undergoing the training and for the library/information service.

Another key element which needs to be built into the training programme is a mechanism for feedback, important for both the trainee and the manager, not only for evaluating the success of specific modules of training, but also to provide the opportunity for (a) problem solving and (b) putting the training into a broader professional context. In the case of the longer-term programme, feedback is likely to take place during regular counselling sessions, an approach endorsed by the Library Association, which also recommends the maintenance of a log-book, enabling the trainee to measure their own progress.

In drawing up a training programme there are a number of factors which will have to be taken into consideration. First the participants and their *level of operation and ability* – the level to be assessed not only in terms of the post held by each member of staff, but also of earlier formal education and previous experience which may indicate potential as well as ability and could help determine the type of training to be offered. Also relating to the participants will be the *training methods* to be applied in relation to predicted different responses by individuals, given their varied *learning styles*. As mentioned earlier, some respond better to what they hear, others to what they see, some work well in groups, others are better on their own. In addition the *timing and pacing of the training* should be set with the individual in mind. Other considerations include the *organizational and departmental developments* to which the training will need to relate; the *sequence and logical flow* of the programme and the availability of *in-house programmes, facilities, materials and skills* which could successfully be made use of, and adequate *budgets* for the purchase of external elements, whether these are visits requiring travel expenses, courses with a fee to be paid, or reading matter and software to support internal activities.

These then need to be added to the identified training needs of the individual in order for the programme to take shape. In what areas is training likely to be needed?

The range could probably be summarized under several main headings:

- The front end, i.e. direct dealing with users/clients
- The acquisition and organization of resources
- Information handling (organizing and retrieving)
- Management
- Administration.

However, there is inevitably a degree of overlap, for example the front end would cover aspects of service provision such as enquiry handling, loan services and user education. These in turn are dependent on information handling, administrative and interpersonal and communication skills, the latter including telephone techniques as well as written and face-to-face communication. These skills are also used in the reference interview, in conducting user surveys, the provision of current awareness services and the dissemination of information generally, as well as in promotional activities. They are also essential to the manager's own role in staff management, negotiation and other internal and external activities. Training in other management areas, for example time management, needs to be available to all staff if an effective service is to be maintained, meeting deadlines and handling procedures efficiently.

When deciding on the most appropriate training activities for a programme, the complex mix of skills required for the successful execution of work tasks will be central to your considerations. It is therefore worth subjecting each area of operation in the department to regular assessment – is it still necessary, how well is it being performed, how could it be improved? This will provide a method of identifying training needs at a departmental and service level, while contributing to personal efficiency and quality assurance.

References

1. Webb, S. P. (1991) *Personal development in information work* 2nd edn. London: Aslib.
2. Webb, S. P. (1991) *Best practice?: continuing professional development for library/information staff in UK professional firms.* British Library R & D Report 6039. Berkhamsted: Sylvia P. Webb.

CHAPTER TWELVE

Quality assurance and performance measurement

Efficiency, effectiveness, flexibility and managing change all form part of an area of increasing interest to LIS managers, and to their employing organizations, namely, the concept of quality assurance. This important area needs to become an integral part of providing any type of library and information service, kept at the forefront of the minds of all those involved, but particularly the manager. He or she will have responsibility for setting up mechanisms whereby quality in an LIS context can be defined and discussed, with full staff involvement, and monitoring procedures put into place to ensure that quality of service is consistent and of a high standard. Quality is as dependent on the human resource element of library and information provision as it is on the information itself and its supporting systems. Therefore, staff attitudes and skills form an essential part of quality as perceived by the users of the service, calling for considerable leadership from the manager if a policy of quality assurance is to be successfully implemented. As illustrated by the Aston case study which follows, quality-related LIS activities are likely to be part of an overall organizational strategic plan, which includes a policy of quality assurance, so it is essential that the manager consults with appropriate contacts in the organization to ensure that a coherent approach is taken. However, in addition to quality of service it is equally important for the manager to seek quality in all forms of training and development. In 1988 the Council of the American Library Association adopted guidelines put forward by the Continuing Education Subcommittee of its Standing Committee on Library Education (SCOLE) [1]. These set out a comprehensive list of criteria by which to assess the quality of different types of continuing education programmes and activities, and are well worth careful consideration.

An interesting example of the introduction of a quality assurance programme into a special library is described by Anne M. Fredenberg [2] in her capacity as Director of the Kubie Medical Library at the Sheppard and Enoch Pratt Hospital in Baltimore, Maryland, USA. In her article, Fredenberg also offers ten helpful suggestions for managers who may be about to start out on the process of establishing a quality assurance programme for their library or information department. The library's move towards quality assurance (QA) was part of an institution-wide programme which required departmental managers to spend 1 year developing guidelines and becoming familiar with the systematic methods and record-keeping involved. Fredenberg describes the administrative focus as being on the process, which includes setting goals, analysing current activities, identifying problems, setting priorities, implementing changes, periodic evaluation, and consultation with administration, all of which suggest a number of areas in which the manager may need to develop or improve certain groups of skills such as communication, planning and leadership.

Performance indicators have a valuable part to play in the overall assessment of service quality, as was found at Aston University in the UK. Christine Abbott, who managed the project, talked to me about it, and in particular its implications for LIS management development.

Case study: Performance indicators in Aston University's Library and Information Services

The project came about initially as an immediate response to a call from senior management to all departments of the university for increased efficiency and effectiveness. This was in the wake of a radical and comprehensive restructuring aimed at positioning the university as a leading technological institution and centre of excellence. Christine noted that, although performance indicators were introduced in many academic libraries in response to national directives and cost-cutting exercises, at Aston the main interest was not primarily that of justifying resources but of developing improved management tools. Whilst realising that performance indicators on their own would not con-stitute better management, they were seen as having considerable potential in terms of improving the quality of management and decision making by providing managers at all levels with the information they needed to make decisions. This particular project was therefore seen as part of a broader exercise of organizational planning, aimed at achieving change to realign the Library and Information Services (LIS) with the new objectives of the university.

High-quality management and skilful financial planning, alongside strong leadership, were essential, and the whole project was underpinned by quantitative systems of assessment to ensure efficiency and effectiveness. At the senior university level a management development programme was adopted to improve and develop appropriate expertise to make sure that the skills necessary to the success of the project were in place. At the start of the project in LIS it was essential to establish just where the performance indicators stood in the planning process, and quite a lot of time was spent in identifying the focus of such a planning strategy. Given that the LIS plan was part of a larger overall strategy, it was essential that performance indicators were seen in relation to both departmental and organizational medium- and long-term objectives. In terms of the LIS objectives, performance indicators had to be viewed as an integrated part of staff development, service provision and customer care.

Christine states the four major objectives of the project as being:

- To develop a series of performance indicators to be used as management tools at all levels
- To explore ways of obtaining better management information from the GEAC computer system
- To review and revise LIS operational statistics
- To develop unit and service costings, primarily as efficiency indicators for use in resource planning and comparative analysis between libraries, and to assist in the university-wide process of bidding for student numbers.

Although the concept of performance indicators was a relatively new one to most of the library staff, a number of measures had already been taken which helped staff to view this as a natural and positive development. A range of development activities and projects under way meant that staff were already involved in activities designed to give the more proactive and service-oriented approach being sought. A university-wide training programme was also developing a corporate culture based on customer care, and this had been enthusiastically adopted by the library staff.

A crucial first step, which proved a very wise one, was to appoint on to the staff a full-time Planning Assistant, rather than rely on the services of an external consultant. This had a major impact on the way in which the project was viewed by LIS staff, that is, they were able to build a positive relationship with someone who was very much part of the team. For example, the Planning Assistant took turns, along with all the library professionals, to staff the Information Point (Enquiries Desk). As well as providing her with valuable insights into customer needs and the LIS service focus, this move helped her to be seen as a fully integrated member of LIS staff, sharing the professional responsibilities of her colleagues.

It was seen as most important to have full staff involvement and support, as without it the project would be likely to founder and not bring the hoped-for long-term benefits to the LIS, or ultimately to the university. In this, the Planning Assistant acted as a catalyst for change, encouraging managers to consider alternative approaches to problem-solving while at the same time not imposing any particular solutions. Seminars and workshops were organized in which the Planning Assistant as facilitator aimed to focus the staff on current problems and issues. Performance indicators were presented as a means of informing decisions on how to tackle management problems.

The procedure used to develop performance indicators for each service is set out in Fig. 12.1.

A 'bottom up' approach was adopted whereby solutions to managers' individual concerns were sought within the process as it developed, rather than imposing perhaps less precise solutions by working downwards from an all-embracing scheme. By first agreeing a common purpose, the staff themselves were encouraged to put forward suggestions, ideas for improvements, and the performance indicators relevant to their areas of work. Specific targets were not imposed from outside, but emerged through the process of determining and operating the performance indicators. Two particular areas in which performance indicators were introduced were (a) the cataloguing throughput, and (b) the inter-library loan service. Both brought to light the fact that pro-cedural changes and more flexible managerial decisions were needed to ensure the efficiency and effectiveness of these services. Staff were encouraged to use office automation skills to produce spreadsheets for

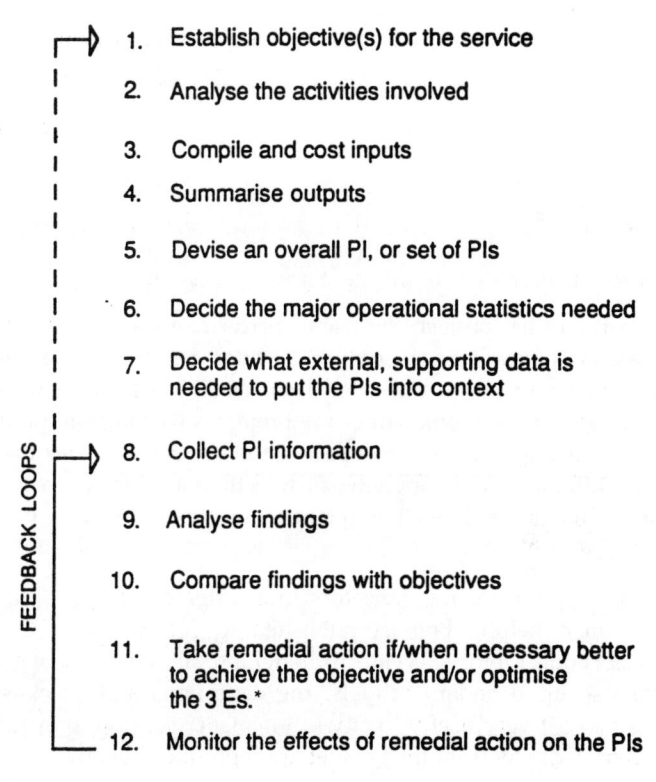

APPROACH TO DEVELOPING AND USING PIs

1. Establish objective(s) for the service
2. Analyse the activities involved
3. Compile and cost inputs
4. Summarise outputs
5. Devise an overall PI, or set of PIs
6. Decide the major operational statistics needed
7. Decide what external, supporting data is needed to put the PIs into context
8. Collect PI information
9. Analyse findings
10. Compare findings with objectives
11. Take remedial action if/when necessary better to achieve the objective and/or optimise the 3 Es.*
12. Monitor the effects of remedial action on the PIs

FEEDBACK LOOPS

Fig. 12.1 Approach to developing and using PIs

*Economy, efficiency, effectiveness

Reproduced by kind permission of Aston University Library and Information Services.

maximum analysis of the data, and computer graphics for informative presentation, for example the calculation of delays occurring at each stage of an activity, the production of a series of graphs. Priorities were established for different activities, for example which items should be catalogued first; targets were set based on the analysis of current performance and future possibilities, e.g. acceptable delivery times for inter-library loans.

Key management points that arose out of the project as a whole were:

- The central role performance indicators can play in the staff development process
- The importance of systematic management of information gathered during such a project

and above all

- The interrelated nature of different areas of service.

Following the initial project, the use of performance indicators in the LIS at Aston is now seen as part of a wider activity of operational planning, as a tool in the quest for Total Quality Management. One clear message that has come out of the project is that knowing how to use performance indicators is just part of the portfolio of skills needed by today's LIS manager in applying such techniques. Many other skills relating to qualitative as well as quantitative aspects of their use are required.

The use of performance indicators in a different sort of library is described in a helpful booklet published by Hertfordshire County Council's Schools Library Service. Although produced as a set of guidelines for use in secondary schools, the definitions and checklists it provides make it very useful to any LIS manager seeking to introduce the concept. Extracts from the booklet are reproduced below:

HOW TO USE PERFORMANCE INDICATORS
They can be used:

- by the librarian for the review and development programme
- as a checklist to assess the current state of provision to ascertain what can be developed quickly and economically
- to identify contacts to be made
- to highlight areas for long-term improvement

- for annual assessment to evaluate progress made over the previous twelve months
- to collate results for an annual report to the Senior Management Team of the School; Governors and Parent Teachers Association
- to assist in future planning, development and spending

TARGET STATEMENTS FOR THE LIBRARY

The target statements are linked directly to the aims and specific objectives for development and are in no particular order.

Accommodation and Ambience
- There is an attractive working environment.

Access
- The library is open before, during and after the school day to all staff and students.

Guiding
- This should facilitate easy use of the library, and be accurate, clear and professional looking.

Stock
- Appropriate and accurate stock in good condition covering the school's curriculum and recreational needs.

Staffing
- The library is professionally staffed on a full-time basis with clerical support. This will enable students and staff to make maximum use of the resources and information.

Funding
- To maintain and improve the school library in terms of space, furniture, materials and equipment.

Service Provision and Planning
- The school is aware of and exploits all available external agencies as appropriate.

Information Technology
- There are computers in the library used for a variety of purposes.

Policy
- A written policy exists, is agreed and is regularly reviewed.

Promotion
- Active promotion of the library and its resources to all staff and students occurs.

Information skills
- An agreed information skills policy exists, and is reviewed in line with curricular need.

Cross Phase Liaison
- Awareness of the current information skills practised in feeder primary schools and knowledge of the skills required for students' future needs. This ensures a progressive approach to life skills.

Monitoring and Evaluation
- Library performance is systematically evaluated to ensure effective delivery and potential.

[The booklet then continues by setting out a number of detailed criteria under each heading, beside which there are two columns headed OPTIMUM and MINIMUM under which the stage of achievement of each criterion is noted. This will provide a detailed overall plan and indicate where most resourcing and effort will be required to ensure that targets are met. It will also indicate the line for future planning.]

(Reproduced from *If you can't measure it, you can't manage it: performance indicators for secondary schools* [3] by kind permission of Hertfordshire County Council's Schools Library Service.)

The performance being assessed may be that of the individual, the service or the organization as a whole. Each will have an impact on the other areas being assessed. Good management practice involves the constant review of all aspects of the service to ensure not only that objectives are being met, but that the objectives themselves continue to be relevant. If not, they too may need to be modified, one of the suggestions in the CSIRO case study which follows.

Case study: CSIRO

CSIRO (Commonwealth Scientific and Industrial Research Organization) is Australia's foremost scientific research and development enterprise in terms of the scale, diversity and quality of its research activities, and because of the consequent benefit to Australia of those activities. CSIRO's main role is to conduct strategic research to develop technologies for all sectors of Australian industry; to improve the management of Australia's natural resources; to protect Australia's unique environment; and to promote the well-being of the Australian people. In corporate sector terms, CSIRO is a conglomerate of 32 individual 'companies' organized into 6 major industry-oriented groups. It has a total staff of about 7000 spread across Australia. CSIRO's role in Australian research and development is particularly significant because it undertakes a large proportion of government-funded R & D, and consequently, a large proportion of all R & D in Australia. CSIRO's Information Services Unit coordinates and supports a network of regional site libraries and is heavily involved in database development, as well as carrying out a range of other LIS activities, including the organization of a considerable collection of scientific material. LIS staff, along with all other departments, participate in the organization's Performance Planning and Evaluation scheme, introduced in 1991. The scheme was publicized to staff through a series of meetings at every site and by the circulation of the following article in the staff newsletter:

PERFORMANCE PLANNING AND EVALUATION: the wheels of progress and how to ride them.

A new method of assessing the work of CSIRO staff members comes into force on July 1 this year – Performance Planning and Evaluation, or PPE, to its friends. Below is a brief account – based on information supplied by the Human Resources Branch – designed to give CoResearch readers a glimpse of what's in store.

The CSIRO's new Performance Planning and Evaluation program aims at top quality work, including leadership, linked to improved career planning and development. The system will follow a yearly cycle, with the appraisal period beginning in May and winding up in June the following year. Here's how it goes.

STAGE 1 – setting the performance objectives and development plan

You begin by listing your job responsibilities on the PPE form and giving it to your manager. The two of you then get together for a formal planning discussion with specific tasks:

- Working out a personal development plan.

This is to give you and your manager a basis for career planning and development activities. You simply write down your career preferences and your development and training priorities.

- Clarifying work activities and responsibilities.

You do this by writing down your broad functions, your work activities, and your areas of responsibility within your programme. These will, of course, be related to the programme objectives, so this is the time to clarify these with your manager.

- Setting work objectives

This is to make sure you and your manager have the same idea about exactly what work you are to get done during the appraisal period, and how that work will be evaluated. That is, which activities are the key ones on which your performance will be judged; your work objectives should be specific about both the quantity and the quality of the results expected from you in key areas of the job.

- Recording your 'competencies'

This simply means copying in the 'competencies' that are listed as expected at your classification level. The question of whether they actually match your real skills doesn't arise until assessment time. Competencies are still something of a mystery to most staff at CSIRO, but you will have them in time for your first PPE sessions. In the meantime they could be roughly described as combinations of skill, knowledge and aptitude, as opposed to qualifications. Problem-solving ability, for example, will be one of them, and a CSOF 2 would be expected to have a lower level of that ability, or competency, than a CSOF 3. They will be an important part of your assessment for promotion, and CoResearch will carry an article soon on this part of the new system.

You can take a colleague into this first formal session if you feel uncertain about handling it on your own. When you and your manager have agreed on all this and written it down, both of you sign the form and it is sent off to the next level up, that is, to your manager's manager. With approval at that level, you and your manager can also set down extra training or resources you feel you need to achieve your work objectives.

It's not set in concrete, however. The work objectives and the personal development plan can both be modified during the appraisal period, though all such modifications should be endorsed by the higher level manager. And that higher level manager is also the one who steps in to mediate if you and your manager disagree on what you should write into your PPE agreement at that first meeting.

STAGE 2 – continuing performance review and feedback

This stage goes on for the whole evaluation period, that is all year. The point of it is to make sure that managers have frequent communication with staff members. Your manager should provide you with continuous feedback, monitoring your progress and giving you the encouragement and support you need to achieve your objectives and improve your skills. You and your manager should both keep a 'significant events diary' to try to make sure neither of you falls into the trap of remembering only what you want to remember or forgetting things that happened a long time ago. It's all too easy to let this week's triumph or disaster overshadow the rest of the year's work.

STAGE 3 – completing the appraisal

Like Stage 1, this stage is a meeting between you and your manager, and again, you can have a fellow worker with you if you want to. If the manager has been doing his or her job there shouldn't be any surprises at this meeting, since you'll have been getting continuous feedback on whether your work was satisfactory or not. You should prepare for the meeting simply by summarizing your achievements over the year.

This formal appraisal discussion focuses on a comparison of your achievements and performance with the objectives and competencies you wrote down at the first meeting, or as modified by both of you during the year. There may also be important achievements that are not on that original agreement but should be considered nevertheless.

Your manager should prepare for the discussion by:

- looking back over the achievements noted in the significant events diary;
- if necessary, seeking relevant information from other sources; and
- trying to anticipate what concerns you might want to bring up about your career development and what planned activities for the unit might affect your next appraisal cycle.

By the end of the meeting the two of you should have been able to agree on your overall performance, and this agreement should include an assessment of:

- your achievements, including any special circumstance that affected whether or not, or how well, you managed your agreed work objectives;
- the level of competencies you showed; and
- your development during the period, identifying strengths and/or weaknesses, especially with an eye to your development needs, which can then be incorporated into the personal development plan you prepare at the beginning of the next appraisal cycle.

When you have agreed on all this, your manager will summarize your overall level of performance as 'very good', 'satisfactory', 'fair', or 'deficient'. If appropriate, he or she can then recommend merit awards and, if authorized, approve incremental advancement. With this system increments are no longer automatic, and if your performance is 'fair' or 'deficient' your pay will not rise. But, on the plus side, your manager can reward good performance with any or all of the following:

- accelerated advancement – this will be considered where your work for this year and other years seems to be consistently outstanding;
- incentive payment – where your current year's work seems outstanding; and
- reclassification – where your achievements and competencies seem to justify a higher level.

Whether or not you get an increment will depend on whether or not you have achieved your work objectives and competencies. In some cases, however, your manager may decide that your performance was satisfactory even though you didn't achieve your objectives, judging that the fault lay in circumstances beyond your control, for example, a bushfire may have burned out your experimental plantings, your computer may have broken down repeatedly, or you may have had an unusual amount of time off with sickness. Or, as often happens, the task you were working on may have opened up like a flower, revealing undreamt-of complexities.

In all of this, if you and your manager don't see eye to eye, you move to the next-up manager.

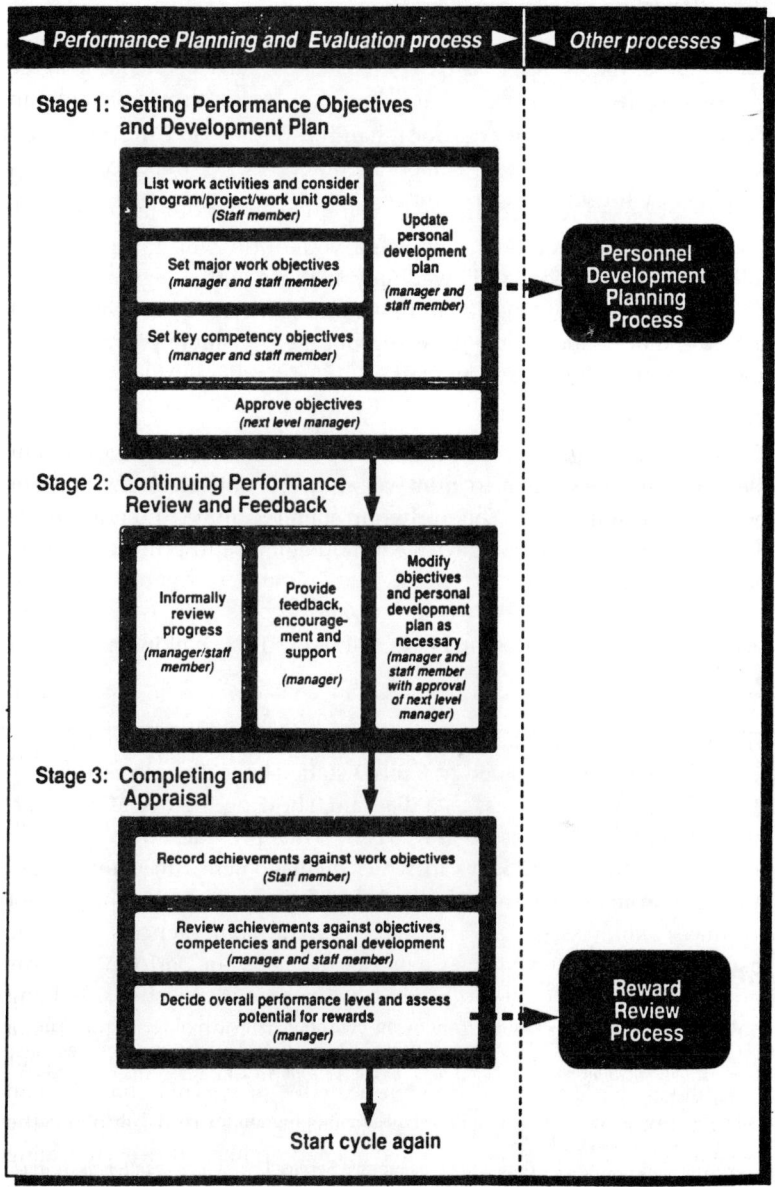

Fig. 12.2 Performance planning and evaluation process

Reproduced by kind permission of CSIRO

Confidentiality

Your manager will keep your form handy, so that you can have access to it whenever you like, but will not let others see it. You, of course, can keep a copy for your own reference.

As each appraisal cycle is completed your form will go onto a confidential file, with access allowed only to those with a legitimate right, as verified by the Divisional Personnel Officer or equivalent. (In practice, that would normally be appropriate Divisional personnel staff and appropriate management staff.)

The next cycle

The next cycle begins as soon as the old one is complete, but you might like to take a few days to think about work objectives for the next period, and that's fine. You and your manager would then arrange a good time for another Stage 1 meeting, beginning the process for the next appraisal period.

(Reproduced from CoResearch, No. 340, May 1991, by kind permission of CSIRO.)

The information contained in the above article was presented as a leaflet which was circulated to CSIRO staff. The leaflet also set out the three stages of the process as a diagram, showing their relationship to other personnel processes (Fig. 12.2). This provides a very useful example of one of the ways in which management can communicate information in a clear and easy-to-follow format.

References

1. American Library Association Continuing Education Sub-committee of the Standing Committee on Library Education (SCOLE) (1988) *Guidelines for quality in continuing education for information, library and media personnel.* Chicago: American Library Association
2. Fredenberg, A. Quality assurance: establishing a program for special libraries. *Special Libraries*, Fall 1988, 277–284
3. Hertfordshire County Council Schools Library Service (1991) *If you can't measure it, you can't manage it: performance indicators for secondary schools. Hertford: Herts C C Schools Library Service*

CHAPTER THIRTEEN

Training for new staff

Your training programme cannot concentrate solely on existing staff – it also needs to provide for new recruits. Attitudes and approaches developed early in an individual's employment are likely to last, and if not appropriate will be very difficult to remedy later, so a prompt introduction to organizational and departmental norms and procedures is crucial and will require considerable managerial involvement to ensure a consistent set of standards across the department. Other members of the team should also participate in introducing the new recruit to their areas of responsibility and to staff in other departments – it is essential that they should feel involved, and that they are considered by you to have expertise which you want them to pass on. This is good for morale as well as for personal motivation. What must be ensured is that lack of understanding or knowledge does not lead to the new recruit being misinformed.

The induction process

The induction process is a key element in any training programme. Up to the time of appointment the new recruit will have based their perceptions of the organization, the department and the job on the limited information provided during the selection process. Actually becoming part of the organization and carrying out the various aspects of the job is a demanding yet rewarding pursuit, with those initial perceptions broadening and growing out of first-hand experience. It is therefore essential that the information provided is accurate and as detailed as required. The induction process involves the passing on of information about the various functions of the organization, combined with meeting people and establishing what is based where. For the new recruit it is a high learning curve, requiring considerable concentration and questioning to pull it all together. This is where managers play a central role, making themselves readily available to answer questions and, where appropriate, suggesting means by which the new recruit may be able to find out for themselves.

What are the components of an induction programme? The first day's activities should aim at a general familiarization with the new workplace and the job, and in particular should allow the new recruit to establish a base. Having a desk or locker in which to put your personal belongings, as well as a supply of pens, pencils and stationery, is important. Knowing where the cloakroom is, and what the lunch arrangements are, may all sound pretty basic, but once the basics are established the new recruit will feel comfortable and able to concentrate on the wider issues involved. It is good practice to give the new recruit one or two tasks on that first day, so that they will be able to end the day with a feeling of having achieved something and made a contribution – they will feel that they have really started. A mini-tour is appropriate at this stage, pointing out key areas of which early cognizance is helpful. Limit the number of personal introductions at this stage, to allow new members of staff more easily to remember faces and names. In some organizations photographs of staff are displayed on a notice board, often for security reasons; these can also form a useful point of reference for the new recruit, as can any brochures which may contain photographs and organization charts. The internal telephone list can also be useful in staff identification, especially if it is arranged both by department and personal name. Make sure that the new member has their own copy.

Most organizations require the first portion of the day to be spent with the personnel department, clarifying conditions of employment, providing any relevant documentation and establishing personal details for the records. General discussion about company training policies may take place here, but the specifics of the individual's training are more likely to be discussed with the line manager. It is with this person that the next part of the day is likely to be spent. The manager or supervisor should set the job in perspective and introduce the new member to the rest of the staff, having first provided the opportunity for the new recruit to put away personal belongings, note his or her extension number and generally establish a base. The manager will outline the structure of the organization and describe the main activities of the department before moving on to the role that the new recruit has been appointed to perform. Any supporting documentation such as guides to the service or organizational brochures should be given to the new member for retention and later reference. At this stage it is probably advisable to hand new staff over to a colleague, carefully selected in advance, to take them around the department and talk less formally to other colleagues about the service. The new member will also be gaining information by observation, for example of the layout, the information resources and the general style of behaviour towards users of the service. It can be reassuring for someone on their first day in a job to recognize familiar sources or equipment, and to be able to establish some early credibility with their new colleagues by being encouraged to participate in dialogue rather than being subjected to a non-stop listing of 'what we have' and 'here is' – hence the need for careful selection of the member of staff who is to conduct this initial walkabout.

The department must be able to continue to function throughout this process, so it is a good idea at some stage of the day to introduce the tasks you want the new recruit to carry out. Make sure that these are described clearly, along with any relevant sources or procedures, including any manual of procedures which exists, encouraging the individual to use it for reference at all times; at the same time impress on them your willingness and that of the rest of the team, to be consulted throughout. Make sure that the new member of staff is not suddenly abandoned at the midday break: perhaps the colleague who was given earlier responsibility could offer to show them the staff dining area, or the nearest sandwich bar, and describe nearby shopping facilities. Most library and information services operate continuously throughout the day, covering breaks on a shift or rota basis. It is important to involve new recruits in decisions about their place in the rota, for example if there is a choice of taking late or early lunch encourage them to be honest in stating their preference, especially where this may be based on the need to meet a prior commitment. This is best established in the discussion with the supervisor or manager, rather than risking other members of staff unwittingly putting their preferences to the fore. It is particularly important where flexible schedules and job-sharing arrangements are involved.

The first afternoon could allow the new recruit to continue with the tasks which have been allocated, followed by an introduction to one specific section of the stock/services. It is useful to allow a little time for constructive browsing, asking questions as they arise, to enable the recruit to become familiar with the sources available. It is important that they do not feel superfluous or forgotten, so suggest that at the end of that time they make contact again with you or another member of staff to move on to the next part of the schedule. You may want to fit in another short walkabout, or send them off to deliver something to a department to which they were introduced earlier. Before the end of the day you should have a meeting to summarize their activities, to provide feedback on the completed tasks, to answer any questions, and to set expectations for the next day, according to the programme that you will have given them at the beginning of the day. The balance of tasks, visits and introductions will shift as familiarization takes place and the new recruit begins to demonstrate a range of ability. Where you have a standard training programme, this demonstration of understanding and ability will indicate to you when to introduce specific training activities, but before this it is advisable for the recruit to participate in any formal centrally organized induction course, often involving all new employees, whatever their specialist function or level.

Depending on the organization, these may be run several times a year, or just whenever there is a suitable number of new recruits. In a commercial organization the induction course will usually involve one or two days away from the department, following a structured programme during which new staff will meet each other and be given a series of short presentations by senior members of other departments. These are usually intentionally informal, often offering the opportunity for the presenters to talk further with the new recruits over lunch, answering questions and just generally making them feel at home with the organization and each other. From the new employees' viewpoint they will suddenly have a series of personal contacts as well as knowing more about the organization and the way in which it operates.

The pace at which the total induction process is taken is important, as it is very easy to give too much information at a time. Constant questioning and checking by the new member of staff is to be encouraged, and is essential if they are to be expected to follow certain procedures, work to stated standards and become integrated into the department.

The induction process does not end with the formal induction day or course but continues over a period of time, with the initial introductions being taken further through a series of longer and more detailed meetings with heads of various departments or functions. These need to be built in at appropriate stages throughout the longer-term training programme. They need to be arranged in advance, regarded as important and booked into the diary as formal meetings. If two new members of staff can go together, this will be beneficial in that (a) there will be the reinforcing factor of subsequent discussion as well as two sets of notes taken during the session, and (b) it will avoid the need to make too frequent demands on the senior staff involved.

On-the-job training

Apart from the familiarization sessions, staff will also learn by observing other staff. This should be encouraged but make sure that the particular staff member chosen for observation knows how to train as well as being good at their job. This is something to be talked through before the arrival of the new recruit, so that staff can think about and perhaps be advised of possible techniques to use, and make adequate preparation. If well prepared this approach can be very successful, and can also contribute to the establishment of working relationships for the future.

Case study: Westminster Reference Library

Another training method found by Westminster Reference Library (part of a London public library service) to be very successful with new members of staff is that of 'shadowing'. Chris Tighe, currently the Training Officer there, says that the aim is to get a competent member of staff in the shortest possible time, whilst ensuring that they feel comfortable with the learning experience, yet allowing them to make an early contribution to the work of the department. On their first day new members of staff meet the Business Unit Manager for an explanation of the service – how it operates and what is expected of them. They then move on to a general tour of the building, both resources and facilities, with the Training Officer. On the second half of that same day, they are likely to find themselves on the enquiry desk – potentially a daunting prospect. This is when the 'shadowing' begins. The Training Officer stands close by, listening to the enquiry but not interfering with the trainee's communication with the enquirer. When the questioning has finished, the Training Officer talks with the trainee to establish that the question has been interpreted correctly and to suggest an appropriate source in which the answer is likely to be found. He then accompanies the trainee to seek the source material and suggests how best to use it. All this must be handled very discreetly to avoid embarrassment to the trainee, and to avoid a loss of confidence by the enquirer. It has to be carried out fairly quickly too, as the enquirer is usually waiting there for the answer. Chris Tighe stresses the importance of consulting with the trainee and not with the enquirer during this process, so that he is not seen to be interfering or taking over. As the trainee gains in both confidence and knowledge the 'shadow' gradually withdraws. Other elements of early training cover identifying and locating sources, the use of reference works and periodicals, bibliographic checking, and use of the catalogue. Quizzes have been found to be a useful training method in these areas.

Over the first 4 or 5 weeks there will be a series of sessions on specific types of material, for example those dealing with government publications, maps, law, the European Community, all taken by senior members of staff specializing in those fields. The layout of the building in relation to the location of different parts of the reference collection has also been taken into account in structuring the training. For example, the ground floor which houses the commercial and technical material and the catalogues, acts as the key to the whole library. Therefore, trainees carry out their initial training and become fully competent there before moving on to the first floor, which houses general reference material, a much more diffuse collection. Here they receive the next block of training. They then alternate between these two floors regularly, often on a daily basis, to reinforce their early training as well as to widen it. After perhaps 6–9 months, they will move on to further training on the second floor, which houses the art library, and which will involve them in rather more specialist training. The 'shadowing' process has proved especially successful not least because it has been carried out with great sensitivity as well as being handled by someone with considerable experience in reference work.

Chris Tighe offers the following practical hints to managers conducting or contributing to the induction process:

- Draw up checklists to ensure every topic is covered
- Never go straight into a session – spend a little time on non-work matters first

- Never parade your own knowledge
- Sessions should be custom-made for the trainee, not the trainer
- Watch out for signs of fatigue, if necessary terminating the session when saturation is reached
- Don't be too encouraging – they need to realize they still have a long way to go
- Watch for weaknesses, exploit strengths
- Remind and reinforce: e.g. Didn't we look at that on Tuesday? That's very similar to the question we had yesterday.
- Give plenty of feedback, show interest, e.g. How was the last session? Anything you want to go over again? If you think of anything let me know.
- Informal daily consultation is essential.

Wherever possible, 'live' situations should be used in the training process, for example working on real enquiries, carrying out tasks which meet a real need such as developing an index or updating subject files. Not only will the new member feel that they are learning, they will also know that they have made a real contribution. One successful way of doing this is to give the new recruit a project which will be their own special area of responsibility. They will be able to carry it out over a period of time, seeking advice as needed, but also having the opportunity to use their initiative. One approach used in the Stoy Hayward training programme (Chapter 11) was that of setting up an index for the monthly newsletter produced by the technical department. It was something which had long been felt would be useful, and as enquiries emanating from this newsletter grew, it became the project for a new member of staff. It provided a learning situation on indexing techniques, along with the need to talk to potential users about their requirements in respect of such an index. It also required the indexer to build up an understanding of the accounting terms used, which was valuable in the long term, given the nature of the organization and its broader information needs.

Where there is more than one library or information department within an organization, job rotation is another work-based method which can be used as part of training. Job rotation usually operates by providing a short fixed term in each department or role. This in itself means that staff are more motivated to learn in the limited time they know to be available, will not be there too long for everything to become routine or boring, and are therefore likely to bring a fresh approach to the tasks involved. Job exchange, although involving longer periods in the alternative post, will also bring similar benefits.

CHAPTER FOURTEEN

Training activities and methods of training

There are a number of general work activities such as staff meetings, working parties and committees which can encourage learning and the demonstration of initiative . Even if only one member of staff can take part in these, a feeling of wider involvement can be achieved by feedback from the participant through discussion and the circulation of papers, subject to any confidentiality procedures which have to be observed. The learning which can take place in these activities is based not only on acquiring subject knowledge or familiarity with technical processes, but offers considerable opportunity to observe meetings behaviour and to learn what makes it successful – the skills of control and negotiation – and to develop an organizational perspective rather than just a departmental one. This is particularly important in the library and information business, where maximum contributions can only be made by gaining this broader understanding.

Attendance at meetings and membership of working parties and committees usually reflects the LIS department's involvement in, and responsibility for, various central organizational activities, e.g. records management, internal database development and maintenance, certain specialist areas of expertise and knowledge possessed by staff, such as languages, or the specific emphasis of the service, e.g. in regularly monitoring and analysing subject fields related to the organization's pursuit of its objectives.

The training activities used in the Stoy Hayward programme (Chapter 11) included on-the-job training and attendance at meetings as discussed above, as well as visits to other library and information centres, and internal and external courses. These were supported by regular counselling sessions, guided reading and a personal project. Where the candidate was pursuing the Library Association Route to Associateship they were also encouraged to maintain a logbook. This is not only useful as a record from which to start preparation of the required Library Association Professional Development Report for Associateship, it also allows the candidate to monitor and review personal progress. As such it could prove valuable to all trainees, whether or not they are pursuing a professional qualification.

There are a number of useful training techniques and methods, ranging from the formal course involving lectures interspersed with group and individual activities, to task-based training with constant feedback. Some methods will be better suited to certain areas of the programme, e.g. the improvement of presentation skills requires practice and is well suited to the participative approach with use of video or CCTV recording and subsequent analysis of presentations made by individuals to a group. The participative course needs to be in the hands of a skilled and experienced trainer with an understanding of the behavioural considerations, that is, not only of the reaction of others to the presentation itself, but also of the underlying feelings of the person preparing and making the presentation. This, like any other situation in which individuals find themselves highly exposed, has to be handled with extreme sensitivity. Role playing requires similar treatment and any role-playing situation and characters must be carefully thought out in terms of relevance to the participants' needs, with subsequent feedback if its learning objectives are to be met. When either setting up a training course yourself, or considering others which may be available, it could be useful to ask the following initial questions about the training methods/materials which may be employed:

- How will the training be conducted, e.g. on a one-to-one or on a group basis; face-to-face or by remote training; on a 'demonstrate-then-practise' basis; lecture/discussion?
- What range and mix of methods/materials are available?
- Which would be most appropriate given the stated objectives and the identified audience?
- What training skills are required to maximize the effective use of such materials/methods?

There are a number of commonly used methods/materials as listed below:

- Lecture/presentation
- Demonstration
- Participation
- Discussion
- Group activities
- Role playing
- Simulation exercise
- One-to-one training
- Use of manual tasks
- Question sheets
- Puzzles
- Flipcharts
- Black/white boards
- Overhead projector and transparencies
- Carousel and slides
- Data tablet and computer graphics
- Films, videos
- Audio cassettes
- Compact discs
- Computer packages.

Each training method requires you, as the trainer, to consider how to get the most out of it through practice and preparation, so do test it out, preferably with a colleague acting as the audience. That way you will find out what works, and which alternative methods might be appropriate.

Courses – internal and external

Short courses are valuable as a training method not only because they give the trainee the opportunity to be immersed in and concentrate on a particular area of new knowledge for a period of time without distraction, but also because of the benefits of interacting with others in the learning process. This applies to both internal and external courses, both of which bring a number of benefits. For example, working on an internal course with people from other departments between which there has been little previous contact, can add to each participant's knowledge and understanding of the organization. It is also likely to increase and improve communication across departments, increasing the assistance that each can provide to the other and enhancing work relationships.

External courses provide a forum for the exchange of ideas with others who, although representing a variety of different organizations, nevertheless share common experiences. This can suggest new ways of handling situations and procedures, and solutions to problems. External courses also provide networks of contacts for future reference. The purpose and level of external courses should be clearly stated in the course literature, and are vital to the manager in the process of selecting courses. If you want to know more about the emphasis of a specific part of the course, or to discuss the appropriateness of the level at which it is pitched, always ring the course providers, who should be able to clarify these points or suggest a more appropriate course for your purpose. It is also useful to talk to those in other organizations who might have used the courses. Seek their perception of the success or suitability of certain training events, which will be based on the feedback from their attendee in conjunction with their own management observation of the outcome of that piece of training. Short courses vary in format and duration. They may be based on a series of presentations by one or more lecturers, they may include practical work and demonstrations. Their intention could be to introduce new entrants to the LIS profession to the basic skills required; to update experienced LIS workers on various topics; or to provide a means of refreshing those returning to work after a career break.

Visual aids

When preparing training materials, the trainer needs to consider the most effective way of getting the message across. The underlying key is *keep it simple*, and even the most sophisticated equipment can be used to present ideas in a clear and uncomplicated way, but as with all training aids and equipment it is the way in which it is used that dictates its success or otherwise.

The simple rule is always to try to see the visual aid as the audience will see it. For example, all lettering displayed, whether on a flipchart or via transparencies or computer graphics, needs to be clear and large enough.

The overhead projector properly used is a valuable training aid. However, a few basic rules can help: switch it off when changing transparencies – a bright patch of light on a blank white screen can be visually very trying for those facing it. Transparencies can be revealed in their entirety or a line at a time as appropriate. Again, switch off in between each point if discussion is to take place before moving on.

Little and often is the way to impart information, so avoid long groups of words. Make use of colour and try to create materials that are visually pleasing. These simple rules apply to all types of visual presentation.

The inclusion of training films and pre-recorded videos should not be regarded as an easy option to keep the delegates happy, or to avoid the preparation of additional material – like other training material, they are available to be used, not just shown. Such training materials, which quite often illustrate good and bad practice, can form the basis of a number of activities. For example, participants may be asked to observe and make notes of main points for subsequent structured group discussion, which in turn could lead to the group or individuals being required to draw up action plans. Most commercially produced training materials are accompanied by well-designed literature, usually with separate booklets for delegates and course leaders. These frequently include exercises which can be used to bring home the message. Films and videos are often used as case study exercises, placing participants in certain work situations and requiring them to respond by exercising their judgement and coming up with solutions to the problems portrayed.

Group activities

Not all case studies are film-based: a number of the lengthier ones used in management development provide the participants with sets of documents describing the situation to be resolved. The documents act as the starting point for in-depth group discussion, into which role playing or simulation activities may be incorporated. Such activities also bring to light personal skills, abilities and qualities, for example those of leadership, negotiation or problem solving.

Group activities are not limited to use on courses, they also provide a valuable means of constructive discussion within the department, if properly structured. A regular monthly staff meeting will be more effective if there is a pre-stated key issue or topic of interest to be discussed. Staff need to be encouraged both to prepare their thoughts for this and to contribute these at the meeting. Group discussion can help improve ways of handling certain areas of work. Brainstorming has long been recognized as an effective means of problem solving.

One example of the successful and constructive use of brainstorming is in the area of service review. It is quite common for this to place the emphasis on user opinion – after all, the service is there for the users – but don't forget to seek ideas from staff as well. If you are planning to conduct a user survey, why not conduct a similar one among your staff? Hopefully they will already have been involved in the setting up of the user survey, e.g. in the design of any questionnaire or checklist to be used, so it would be a natural next step for them to put their own ideas into place. Each member of staff should start by writing down as many ideas as possible, being encouraged to use their imagination and come up with innovative ideas for taking the service forward, which can include changing existing activities, both in terms of the front-end service offered and the underlying procedures which make it possible, as well as replacing old with new. Then the brainstorming begins as each member of staff puts forward ideas which in turn stimulate others. Brainstorming can be an extremely useful means of staff development and, when used as described above, can considerably aid service development as well.

Independent learning

An increasingly popular and flexible means of offering training and development opportunities is by the use of self-study, often through computer-based learning for specific areas, or through distance learning packages. In the case of some longer courses leading to a particular qualification, they may also provide access to a personal tutor. This will sometimes be on a face-to-face basis, but is often via telephone or written communication. This form of self-driven learning requires considerable commitment and discipline from the trainee, with support and assistance from the manager and the employing organization. Self-study is an appropriate method for both qualification-based courses and other areas of study which make up the process of continuing professional development. The *Best practice* research, cited in earlier chapters, found that although some participants were not always able to get away from the workplace to attend all the courses they would like to, their employers were often willing to purchase self-study material for them, and in some cases to allocate study time for their use. Although such forms of training should not completely replace course attendance, which has many benefits, it does offer opportunities to pursue study which may not otherwise be made available. As with other methods of training there are both advantages and disadvantages: the main advantage is that of flexibility in terms of pacing by the individual to suit their own needs, with the likelihood of strong reinforcement and retention of the learning because of the nature of the process. The main disadvantage is likely to be a feeling of isolation and lack of direction or awareness of progress without the presence of a mentor, again underlining the importance of feedback in any training situation. Appropriate design of distance learning material is therefore crucial to the learning process. Having decided on the likely audience, along with the results required, the author of the package needs to focus on structure and style, aiming for clarity with brevity. Constant review during the preparation will help identify possible problems the student might encounter, and allow provision to be made for these through the use of appropriate teaching techniques. Layout and pre-sentation plays a large part in motivating the student and retaining interest. A useful pamphlet on the subject of distance learning for those working in libraries is that produced by Dale [1] in the Library Associa-tion's series *Guidelines for training in libraries*. This includes some helpful checklists for those who might be planning to actually prepare training material in a form suitable for distance learning, and a list of organiza-tions who would be able to provide further guidance. Haythornthwaite and White's survey [2] of distance learning packages offered by library schools and other institutions in the English-speaking world will act as a good starting point. Although published in 1989, it does provide the means for managers to update the list of what is available by contacting any or all of the many institutions referred to.

Presentation of material

The preparation of any form of training material needs to be carefully thought through, with both the objectives of the training and the needs of the individual in mind. The first step is to establish what appropriate material already exists – there is no point in expending a lot of time and effort, perhaps at the expense of other management activities, in preparing a training package when a suitable one is readily available. Of course you will wish to establish that it is suitable for the particular purpose you have in mind, but it is always worth considering whether it could be adapted to your needs, perhaps in combination with other material. You may find that it presents an aspect of the topic under consideration that you had not thought of covering, but which could usefully be included. Your main criteria are likely to be:

- That it covers the subject to the degree of detail required
- That it is presented at the right level
- That it is well presented and interesting.

Today's sophisticated level of presentation by most media sets high expectations – the amateur video or poorly written document will simply not have credibility in the eyes of the recipient and the training message will certainly be lost. Even apparently simple written communications, such as instructions for the use of equipment, need to be clearly expressed and well set out if they are to be effective. It is often the task of a junior member of staff to prepare labels and notices, but if that person is given no guidance it is unlikely that there will be a consistent standard or style. Yet labels and notices are part of the outward display of the library/information service and as such need to look professional, as well as performing their job of guiding the user. Whether such signs and instructions are good or bad, they will still make an impression, and it is up to you to ensure that these simple but vital tasks are covered by your training programme, bearing in mind that the trainee needs to know why, as well as how.

The standard advice on written communications is to keep it simple, but this does not mean that it is easy or that no training is necessary. Also, it does not follow that only the manager or supervisor is going to be involved in preparing written communications. In the LIS world especially, staff at all levels need to pass on information in written form, e.g. in response to an enquiry; in internal and external correspondence; in the preparation of a newsletter or bulletin. Again instruction is essential if the outcome is to be successful. The key to success in communication lies in being able to put yourself in the recipients' shoes – how are they likely to respond to the communication? Staff receiving training in this area should be encouraged to follow that approach by asking themselves two questions about every written communication:

Does the recipient need it? and Is it in the form that he or she is likely to want it, or that would be most helpful? This will provide a starting point for trainees from which to move on to matters of length and style, on which you will be briefing and guiding them, working through first drafts with them. They should also be encouraged to consult the procedures manual for details of any house-style requirements and to look at examples of various communications serving a similar purpose, perhaps produced by other organizations. A lot can be learned by scrutinizing the variety of styles in which regular library newsletters and information bulletins are produced – the trainee will also be developing their critical ability in noting the aspects that appeal as well as those which would not be appropriate to their own organization.

Writing can also be carried out as a group activity, with significant benefits in terms of job satisfaction, motivation and teamwork, as shown in another example from Stoy Hayward. Having set up the information service, it was appropriate to write a guide for users – mainly employees – describing the range of services which had been developed, with the guide organized in such a way that it could be used as a quick direct source of reference. It was also intended to reproduce it in client booklets so that they too could be made aware of the potential of the firm's information resource as an additional service available to them. Information staff drew up a list of the most appropriate headings, given the purpose of the guide, and then individuals prepared entries on their particular subject areas, which were combined into a single draft document. This was circulated within the department and amendments of style and content agreed at a single meeting. As well as the considerable sense of involvement and satisfaction in the final product, the exercise had also provided some very practical lessons in the preparation of written communications.

The choice of words and the way in which we use them influences all forms of communication, but the written word plays a significant role in the range of activities which make up a library/information service. For example, the preparation of a newsletter or bulletin requires the ability to summarize and present the main points of the items cited in a concise form, yet at the same time making it punchy enough to whet the reader's appetite to follow up the reference and read the original. The skills needed to write in this brief form are also useful for activities such as abstract writing, cataloguing notes, information reports in response to enquiries, or perhaps summaries for any house journal that might exist. Newsletters and bulletins also act as a promotional tool for the LIS, so layout and presentation are other areas in which staff may require training. Short courses containing practical work are invaluable in providing an insight into the basics of various kinds of writing, for example business letters and report writing, but it is important that the individual concerned should have regular opportunities to put their learning into practice, thus improving and developing further.

Cooperative training ventures

This form of interchange is particularly useful between managers in similar organizations who are likely to have comparable training requirements for their staff. It could also lead to the setting up of cooperative training ventures to cover specific areas in which there is a common need. For example, the London-based Accountancy Library and Information Group felt that the specific approach to understanding various financial matters that they were seeking for their staff was not offered by any of the standard courses available. They therefore approached a consultant specializing in financial training and together designed a series of courses tailor-made to their needs, in terms of subject coverage, level, duration, frequency and price. The training programme is divided into four modules each lasting half a day, to allow maximum flexibility for participants to be able to attend. The total package provides fairly comprehensive coverage and, although aimed at new entrants to the subject area, has also been found to fill the gaps for more experienced information officers. The aim is to give sufficient background knowledge of the sources, along with enough understanding and detail of the nature of the information with which participants are likely to be working on a day-to-day basis. The series of modules is run at intervals to meet the needs of the group and is proving to be very successful. This approach to training could well be emulated by other informal self-help groups.

Cooperative training does not have to take place between similar organizations, or even between organizations in the same country. As Alan MacDougall [3] says, 'There seems to be no particular formula which will guarantee the outward success of a co-operative; it does not seem to depend on the size of the co-operative, its mix or its geographical spread'. The book in fact includes case studies of cooperative training ventures between libraries of one type, as well as between libraries of different kinds. MacDougall suggests that one factor which could be crucial to the success of such schemes is the degree of continuity and stability of the organizing committee. Another will be a considerable commitment to training not only by members of the organizing committee but also by their employing organizations. Where there is support from senior management, MacDougall suggests, there are fewer problems in taking the scheme forward.

In describing a range of cooperative projects across Europe, Ian Mowat [4] mentions one venture which involves the libraries of the Universities of Torun and Lodz in Poland, Debrecen and Szeged in Hungary, and Hull in Great Britain, working together on training and staff exchange.

Obviously there will be lessons to be learned by the organizers as well as by the trainees, so before embarking on a cooperative venture, the long-term implications need to be considered.

When the present authors were employed by Westminster City Libraries and Stoy Hayward, respectively, we felt that there was con-siderable scope for some form of joint training even though the organ-izations involved were quite different, i.e. one was part of a local authority and the other a leading firm of chartered accountants in the private sector. What did we feel would be offered to the participants, given the different structure and objectives of each organization, and the fact that each already had a training programme in place? Overall, we felt that trainees would gain a broader professional awareness in terms of appreciating the range of sources and services on offer, the different ways in which these could be provided, and become more aware of the underlying objectives of the organizations involved. This would lead them to appreciate the need for flexibility of approach and a realization that LIS applications could be transferred across sectors.

The trainees involved attended only selected parts of each other's programmes, but experienced considerable benefit in increased aware-ness and understanding which would be applicable to their longer-term career development. Each saw a different user community with different expectations and needs. One notable example where the elements of the Stoy Hayward approach were seen to be directly applic-able to the Westminster situation was in the setting up of what was at that time a new venture for Westminster's Central Reference Library – a subscription-based service aimed at the local business community. Information for Business is now a well-established commercially run service. However, there was at that time a need to consider not only charging for information provided, but all the other aspects of operating commercially: understanding the business environment and its language, as well as its way of working, meeting business expectations as well as deadlines, thinking laterally, viewing each request for information in a wider perspective, seeking new ways of approaching the search for solutions, and of presenting the answers. This needed more than 'we have got all these reference books and databases – let's make money by using them more'. It required not only a thorough knowledge of business sources, but also how to operate in a business context – quite an opportunity for staff development, but one requiring a carefully thought-out training and development programme.

References

1. Dale, S. (1986) *Distance learning. Guideline for Training in Libraries* No.8. London: Library Association
2. Haythornthwaite, J. A. and White, F. C. P. (1989) *Distance education in library and information studies*. British Library Research Paper 50. London: British Library R & D Dept.
3. MacDougall, A. and Prytherch, R. (1989) *Co-operative training in libraries*. Aldershot: Gower
4. Mowat, Ian R. M. (1991) East-west information transfer. *Information Management Report*, May, 11–14.

CHAPTER FIFTEEN

The manager's own training and development

The effective management of training pre-supposes a knowledge and understanding of people and their behaviour in a learning situation; an up-to-date knowledge of the particular field within which the trainee will be operating; an awareness of available training both internal and external, along with the ability to evaluate the appropriateness of that training and the skill to assess its effectiveness, accompanied by any necessary counselling and advice; and experience and knowledge of training techniques and methods. Quite a tall order, and often one which is not thought through in such detail when the appointment of a departmental manager is made. Unfortunately the old adage 'managers are born, not made' is still given credence in some quarters, without consideration that even apparently 'natural' skills can be improved, developed, built on or used differently. Many people, when taking on a library management role, find themselves not just continuing to use their specialist skills and knowledge with 'a bit of administration tacked on', but also regularly being called upon to resolve problems, initiate activities and, in particular, become fully immersed in the whole process of managing financial and human resources as well as those relating to the retrieval of information. In order to carry out those management responsibilities, the newly appointed manager may well require training in various management skills and techniques, as well as being introduced to organizational procedures in which they may not previously have been involved.

'We need managers who are innovative, forward-looking and service-oriented, able to communicate with and get the best out of other people, and skilled in managing resources' – a statement by the British

Library [1], in its strategic 5-year plan aimed at taking the British Library forward to 1994. In that same publication the British Library says that it will pursue staff development by drawing up programmes for each level of management and operation, defining the personal qualities, skills and knowledge essential to each.

It is not only the British Library that is following this line. Libraries and information services of all kinds, in many countries, are recognizing the need for sound management skills if their service is to move forward in line with user demand and at the same time make the most cost-effective use of resources. For example, the opening up of the European Single Market allows freedom of movement by professionals across the job market in all member states. This means that in addition to any specialist knowledge required to carry out a particular job, the benefits of broad-based management skills will help considerably in adapting to any differences there may be in the way in which library and information services are offered.

Being a library or information manager, that is, managing budgets, information, users, staff, and especially top management, requires a wide range of skills. In addition, managers need both creative and analytical skills in order to innovate and plan for a successful future. However, as Margaret Trask, Executive Director of the Australian Information Management Association, said at a seminar on the subject [2] 'managing is usually thrust upon those who show promise in dealing with staff or in getting work done or being competent in their job'. She goes on to suggest that showing promise is not enough; managers needs training and development if they are to realize their full potential in all their areas of responsibility. Trask notes some of the key concerns of those moving from being managed into the process of managing. These include how to motivate staff, managing conflict, setting goals and objectives, and what is described as 'self-concept' or getting to know yourself and to understand your own work behavioural style. As new managers move on to middle and senior management, of course they still have concerns about staff motivation, managing conflict and the areas listed above, but Trask notes that that their main concerns focus on other aspects such as building work groups, negotiation skills, strategic planning and managing change. Other areas of concern to middle and senior managers, also identified by Trask, are lack of trust, power and influence, and leadership. These areas are referred to later in this chapter. The AIMA hopes to publish a Resource

Notebook on Strategic Planning in response to the desire expressed by managers to learn more about planning processes. This need is illustrated in a paper given by Susan Moore to the first national seminar on Library Staff Development held in Australia in 1990 [3]. In this she describes the approach taken in the Royal Melbourne Institute of Technology Libraries when planning a client services programme. One factor that was perceived as being crucial to the hoped-for success of this new direction was staff training, and for that to be effective the plan had to include training for trainers. Training is another area often taken for granted when someone is first promoted to a management position, and yet it requires a considerable range of expertise. Moore's paper provides a useful case study for managers who may be planning a new service or modifying an existing one. It highlights the importance of staff being encouraged to see themselves as part of a team, to have confidence in themselves and their work, and through this to improve service provision and delivery. This will involve the manager in clarifying their role and the objective of the new service, in setting shared priorities, and demonstrating the organizational as well as the individual benefits.

The more responsibility a manager has, the more they need positive and well-defined support from top management. This should be via the two-way communication of new ideas, encouragement to pursue initiatives, trust, clear guidelines, feedback on initiatives taken, and praise when these have been successful and explanation rather than negative reproof if mistakes have been made. An enlightened top management will realize that trust and the freedom to pursue ideas and take action are part of the role of being a professional and a manager, and are vital if creativity is not to be stifled or frustrated. Positive support of this kind can lead to high-level contributions to the organization's goals and objectives by the manager and the service they are running. The development of management potential is a continuing process which, if well-designed and structured, brings maximum benefit to both the organization and the manager.

Staff relations

A motivated manager will lead to motivated staff. In the process of undergoing their own training and development programme, the manager will be much more in touch with what other staff are experiencing, or in need of, regarding their own progress. Their development will give you job satisfaction, while your efforts in your own personal development will not only act as an example for them but also bring about a strong feeling of working together. It will open up communication channels, bring strong team loyalty and lead to service enhancement and development. The British Council case study in Chapter 7 demonstrates the benefits of an organization-wide approach to training and development, and also underlines the direct benefit to staff relations. Good staff relations and understanding are also discussed in Chapter 9 as being central to the effective planning of training to ensure the achievement of its objectives. The induction process described in Chapter 13 is most successful when staff at all levels make a contribution and have ongoing involvement, as was found to be the case in the Westminster City Library case study. Group activities, on-the-job training, appraisal and assessment sessions are all dependent on positive staff relations, based on effective management, as illustrated by the extracts from the Glasgow Employee Assessment and Development Scheme Handbook, reproduced in Chapter 10.

Shared training and joint involvement in a particular area of learning activity can have a strong impact in producing such benefits. For example, the development and introduction of performance indicators and quality assurance programmes described in Chapter 12 shows the potential of such activities in team building. The introduction of various efficiency techniques provides a particularly appropriate area in which to plan shared activity, being something which, to be successful, has to operate consistently across the department and the organization. One such efficiency technique, that of time management, lends itself well to this approach.

Time management

This is another subject on which managers may need to focus in terms of their own development, as well as introducing across the department as a whole. One commodity that is part of everyone's life is time. Unfortunately, unlike most other commodities this one cannot be replaced, nor can an additional amount be purchased. Over recent years there has been a proliferation of management books and articles, as well as seminars and conference papers, devoted to the subject of time and how to use and manage it effectively and efficiently. The main thrust of time management is towards setting up controls to handle more effectively the key elements of our work life, e.g. the physical environment, from the filing system down to the positioning of the desk, and the human factor – people and our interaction with them. 'Never handle a piece of paper more than once' and 'Failing to plan is planning to fail' are two of the maxims regularly put forward, followed closely by firm advice to delegate more. Staff at all levels, regardless of the degree of specialism within which they operate, are likely to suffer from the same conditions, which require them to consider practising more careful time management. Improving time management involves changing behaviour and attitudes. For example, one known time waster is the person – perhaps more senior than yourself – who drops in 'just to see that everything is alright'. How do you convey to them that they have just interrupted a complex thought process concerning a matter they had told you yesterday was top priority? Interruptions feature high on most managers' list of time wasters. Advice on how to deal with them is likely to be included in most time management courses, but you might also be greatly assisted by some assertiveness training. As Helen Gothberg [4] concluded, time management is no longer a case of time and motion study but has rather to do with self-management. She has carried out a number of studies in various types of library including academic [5], special [6] and state [4].

Telephone interruptions and drop-in visitors are ranked second and third on Gothberg's list of top time wasters in special libraries, with the inability to say 'no' coming seventh in the top ten. In state libraries telephone interruptions are again placed as the second-highest time waster, with drop-in visitors fifth and inability to say 'no' eighth. Tom Attwood comes up with a similar list in his article on the subject [7]. He notes lack of focus as the top time waster, with interruptions at number three. It is interesting to compare this with his list of what are considered to be the ten best ways to use time.

Top ten ways to use time	Top ten time wasters
1. Think and plan	1. Lack of focus
2. Establish priorities	2. Poor meetings
3. Get organized	3. Interruptions
4. Be effective	4. Crises
5. Manage change	5. Trivia
6. Adapt culture	6. Procrastination
7. Develop staff	7. Travelling
8. Be practical	8. Failure to plan
9. Use every minute	9. Not delegating
10. Take time off	10. Inappropriate technology

(Reproduced by kind permission of Tom Attwood of Cargill, Attwood & Thomas Ltd.)

The above lists are based on regular analysis of the chief time wasters as indicated by more than 1000 managers in various jobs in 15 countries. Attwood has carried out work of this kind in both companies and professional associations, and is very aware of the need for the development of management skills by those working in specialist fields.

Time management cannot be carried out in isolation. Whatever the organization, whether it be in the public or the private sector, mechanisms need to be put into place to heighten awareness of efficiency potential and to support its pursuit by all members of staff. In order for this to be most effective, each member of an organization needs to be made aware of their own use of time, and have adequate appropriate training in time management skills and techniques, and the opportunity for their continued use. Once the initial promotion and introductory sessions have been carried out on an organization-wide basis, it can then be most beneficial to proceed with the training and development on a team basis within departments, allowing problems and benefits to be shared. This is much more likely to motivate staff to practise time management and not feel uncomfortable about doing so. It is also likely to bring about new ideas on the review of a number of areas of work, ultimately producing a much more effective service to users.

Corporate awareness

It is most important when seeking or setting up any training programme concerned with the introduction of specific concepts and techniques, that these are presented according to the norms and procedures operating across the organization. This will put the training into context and make its application relevant and therefore more likely to be successful. This is when the two-way communication between managers and top management will prove extremely useful. If the organization is planning developments in a certain direction, this will also present additional opportunities for staff development. Attwood points out the importance of managers understanding the company culture, so that when they set about establishing a culture of achievement within their particular department or function, it will be much more likely to work. His article [8] explains how to identify an existing organizational culture and how to use it successfully, or even change it. Among a number of areas influenced by corporate culture, Attwood notes particularly the impact on recruitment, training and development policy, and says that 'a good culture creates loyalty with both staff and customers' and 'it certainly governs the success of any change'. Working with the corporate culture does not mean just conforming or being afraid to introduce change, but rather seeking to make positive use of and build on what is already there. In terms of training and development this is likely to mean identifying the degree of commitment to, and attitudes towards, such activities, as well as establishing what policies exist and how they are currently implemented. Knowledge of these aspects of organizational behaviour will provide you with the appropriate platform from which to launch your own ideas, and help you to project them in the right direction. Lyn Currie [9] notes the importance and potential benefit of viewing staff training and development activities in an organizational context. She says 'there must be visible meaningful support for staff development with an administrative framework that assists with the organization, delivery, management and promotion of staff development activities'. She goes on to give examples of ways in which appropriate support mechanisms can be put into place, one of which is the 'use of interdepartmental working parties to enhance understanding of the interrelationship of library operations' – another example of the way in which two-way communication could enhance the LIS manager's own learning and development.

This emphasis on the importance of developing corporate awareness in conjunction with management skills is strongly supported in the UK by the Library Association in its *Framework for continuing professional development* [10]. In this, four key elements which make up LIS work are identified:

- Library and information skills
- Personal effectiveness/communications
- Management skills
- Corporate skills.

Under the last two headings a number of specific areas are listed as potential areas for continuing professional development. These are:

Management skills	Corporate skills
• Planning	• Achieving goals and objectives of parent organization through library and information services
• Finance/budgeting	
• Personnel/staff management	• Using the organizational context
• Leadership	• Awareness of national and local policies
• Marketing	
• Performance review	• Political know-how

(Reproduced by kind permission of the Library Association.)

The areas of skill and knowledge shown under the heading 'Personal effectiveness' cover problem solving, communications, coaching and teamwork and therefore form an essential base from which to put into practice the above listed management and corporate skills. These certainly underline the broader perspective in which librarians and information managers today and in the future need to view their role, and are very much in line with Attwood's thinking, as mentioned earlier.

Peter Senge [11] is one of a growing number of experts across the USA and in Europe promoting the concept of 'the learning organization'. Among the key elements which make up this concept are those of (a) shared vision which will lead to commitment rather than compliance, and (b) team learning, of which Senge is also a proponent. Another interesting point in Senge's thesis is that he sees the effective leader not as the brilliant orator able to mesmerize an audience, but as someone distinguished by clear thinking, strong commitment to the organization, and enthusiasm to continually learn more.

Effective leadership

Strong leadership as the key to the future success of the LIS profession is well argued by Martha Boaz in her contribution to IFLA's guidebook on continuing education [12]. In this she suggests that not only are dramatic local, national and international changes essential if the profession is to grow, but also that there is a need for more aggressive and productive leaders in the profession.

Library and information professional associations throughout the world are increasingly putting good management to the forefront of their training and development statements and activities, and leadership features increasingly in professional development programmes. As long ago as 1970, the Council of the American Library Association adopted a policy statement on library education and personnel utilization [13]. In this document are listed categories of library personnel, along with the nature of responsibility held by those in each category. It is interesting to note particularly what is said about professional responsibilities, i.e. that they include 'those of management, which requires independent judgement, interpretation of rules and procedures, analysis of library problems, and formulation of original and creative solutions for solving them'. The skills and knowledge required to carry out those responsibilities certainly need to be sought and developed by the individual, but will prove of immense benefit to the library or information department in which they are employed, as well as to the employing organization at large. Thomas Wilding [14], in discussing career and staff development, says that 'when a library takes inventory of its resources, it needs to measure the abilities and skills of its staff as a major asset'. He goes on to say that 'an effective staff development program will broaden the talent and skills base of the staff, providing the library with greater potential for the accomplishment of its goals'. This is yet another indication of the importance to individual library or information managers of developing corporate awareness so that they can themselves pursue, as well as set up for their staff, appropriate training and development activities relevant to the organization's needs.

The Special Libraries Association (SLA) of the USA has been emphasizing the importance of and promoting the effective development and use of management skills to their members for many years, constantly changing the focus to meet current needs and to enable managers to deal with changes of all kinds. In particular, the need for strong and effective leadership is receiving increasing attention from both individuals and associations. A quick glance at the programme for the SLA's 1992 conference reveals both formal papers and personal development sessions on the subject. Over recent years the SLA's journal *Special libraries* has included a number of articles underlining leadership as the key both to the successful running of library and information services and to the future of the LIS profession at large. In one of these Susan DiMattia [15], in reviewing management literature on the subject of leadership, found a number of ideas which could have been articulated with the LIS profession in mind, particularly those relating to the power of information. It is suggested that as organizations cannot develop strategies to take themselves forward without having the appropriate knowledge, information professionals could, if they worked at it, take on leading strategic roles within their organizations.

Elizabeth Orna [16], in looking at the way in which the flow of information is used and managed within organizations, also suggests a link between the power of information and the need for leadership. She sees the role of the information professional as crucial to the development of organizational information policies, thereby identifying another area in which leadership skills would be essential. Leadership is not just about taking your own department, staff and service forward: it also involves stepping outside your particular specialist function and taking an organizational stance; putting forward ideas backed by ways in which they might be implemented for the benefit of the whole organization; acting as a catalyst.

The principal objective of the Australian Information Management Association (AIMA) as listed in its Information Brochure is 'to improve the standard of library management in Australia'. The AIMA puts considerable emphasis on training events and its 1992 list of programmes includes 4 days on leadership effectiveness which centres on the work of the long-established management author Warren Bennis. Each day covers different aspects of management which together provide the skills required for effective leadership. These are outlined below:

- Management of attention – vision, focus, agenda setting and
  futures

- Management of meaning – internal and external development implications; political, social and economic applications
- Management of trust – values clarification, team building, empowerment, communication
- Management of self – self-assessment and development, personal and organizational action plans

Another related AIMA course looks at the management of organizational change and risk taking, while self-management is additionally dealt with in a separate 2-day workshop.

Why the emphasis on leadership? Because managing is not just about organization and administration, it involves that key resource – people. Leadership is about team building, motivating, encouraging and inspiring your staff, innovating, taking the library/information service forward. It also involves using your skills to play a leading role within the organization as a whole, as well as within the department. Among the numerous works on leadership, there are several practical guides to help you improve your skills in this area. *Learning to lead* [17] was written with just that aim in mind; it is very readable and contains a number of practical exercises and case studies which could be applied to a range of different management settings. Another practical guide is *Positive leadership: how to build a winning team* [18], which could act as a useful model for many types of organization.

Continuing to develop

The above discussion has indicated the breadth of skills and understanding needed by today's library or information manager. This has also been clearly illustrated in the case studies and examples given. In particular, the two checklists suggested for use in Sections 4 and 5 of the Glasgow Employee Assessment and Development Scheme provide a useful summary of those attributes which help staff to perform well.

The acquisition of wide-ranging management skills is recognized as being essential in a variety of different types of LIS settings and in many countries. In 1989 Rannveig Egerdal Eidet [19] commented on the beginning of a noticeable trend in Norwegian public libraries, and says that 'matters connected with organization and management have been pushed to the top of the agenda within the national public library system'. He goes on to describe the major management development programme which was at that time being introduced for chief municipal librarians which he says 'aims to enhance the competence of chief librarians – both as leaders of personnel and as leaders within municipal administrative systems'. He points out certain aspects of the public library system which require specific management treatment. For example, he notes that most libraries have few staff and short opening hours, which means that service to the public has to go before planning and more goal-oriented activities. Other priorities can then suffer as a result.

Jean Michel's interesting paper on LIS education and training in France [20] notes the importance of continuing education to ensure the updating of knowledge and know-how of French professionals. He also sets out reasons for changes in both initial and continuing education which he suggests have become necessary through increased international competition and market globalization; a Europe without frontiers, the 'intelligence revolution', and information and communication technologies. He also puts forward a new typology of professional qualifications and functions. These ideas together provide the basis for an LIS education and training model crossing sectors, subjects and national boundaries.

Continuing professional development (CPD) is essential for individuals at all levels if service objectives are to be met. CPD is just as necessary for the library assistant without professional qualifications as for the qualified and experienced senior LIS practitioner. Cruz and Santos [21] point to the need for appropriate training for non-graduate assistants in libraries and documentation centres in Portugal, and describe the efforts made by the professional associations there to establish courses of this kind. Working to professional standards is as important to the employer as it is to the individual practitioner. The *Best practice* report [22] noted that internal and external issues affecting employing organizations were viewed by LIS staff as identifying areas for their own CPD. This often leads to LIS staff seeking their CPD in subjects outside the LIS field, for example in commercial subjects, as was discovered by Pors [23] in his research into employment patterns in Denmark. This was also the case in several Australian business libraries [24].

Studying for a higher degree, within or outside the LIS field, research, writing, lecturing and conducting training all offer considerable opportunity for CPD. Involvement in a variety of professional activities, e.g. participation in subject interest groups, can bring personal development through interaction with other practitioners, stimulating fresh ideas and providing new perspectives.

CPD refers to a range of activities aimed at developing and enhancing knowledge, skills and attitudes. It prepares the individual to carry out their job in the most effective way, increasing motivation and contributing to their long-term progress and achievement. In the hands of an effective manager CPD will ensure not only that manager's personal development, but also that of all their staff, as well as the long-term development and success of the service.

References

1. British Library (1989) *Gateway to knowledge: the British Library strategic plan 1989–1994*. London: British Library Board
2. Trask, M. (1989) Managed, managing and management: life after library school. *AIMA Newsletter*, October, 3–12
3. Moore, S. (1990) Planning for a client services program at Royal Melbourne Institute of Technology Libraries. In *Library staff development: proceedings of the first national seminar, July 1990* (ed. J. Hiscock). Adelaide: South Australian College of Advanced Education
4. Gothberg, Helen M. (1991) Time management in state libraries. *Special Libraries*, Fall, 257–266.
5. Gothberg, Helen M. and Riggs, Donald E. (1988) Time management in academic libraries. *College and Research Libraries*, **49**(2), March, 131–140
6. Gothberg, Helen M. (1991) Time management in special libraries. *Special Libraries*, Spring, 119–130
7. Attwood, T. (1987) Time ticks on and on. *Accountancy*, June, 75–77
8. Attwood, T. (1990) Corporate culture: for or against you? *Management Accounting*, January, 26–29
9. Currie, L. (1990) Management style, decision making and staff development in college libraries. In Hiscock, J. (ed.) *op. cit.*
10. Library Association (1991) *A framework for continuing professional development*. London, Library Association
11. Senge, Peter (1991) *The fifth discipline – the art and practice of the learning organization*. New York: Doubleday
12. Boaz, Martha (1991) The library and information science profession: anticipation of future important changes, local, national, international. In *Continuing professional education: an IFLA guidebook* (ed. B. Woolls) Munich: K G Saur
13. American Library Association (1970) *Library education and personnel utilization*. A statement of policy adopted by the Council of the ALA, June 30
14. Wilding, T. L. (1989) Career and staff development: a convergence. *College and Research Libraries News*, November, 899–902
15. DiMattia, S. (1990) Leadership can be learned. *Special Libraries*, Spring, 126–131
16. Orna, E. (1990) *Practical information policies: how to manage information flow in organizations*. Aldershot: Gower

17. Heim, P. and Chapman, E. N. (1990) *Learning to lead*. London: Kogan Page
18. Pegg, M. (1989) *Positive leadership: how to build a winning team*. Leeds: Lifeskills Publishing Group
19. Eidet, R. E. (1989) Better management – better libraries. *Scandinavian Public Libraries Quarterly*, **22**(4), 20–25
20. Michel, J. (1990) Education and training of information professionals in France. *Libri*, June, 135–152
21. Cruz, M. J. and Santos, M. O. (1990) Education and training of library and information professionals in Portugal. *Libri*, June, 165–168
22. Webb, S. P. (1991) *Best practice?: continuing professional development for library/information staff in UK professional firms*. British Library R & D Report 6039. Berkhamsted: Sylvia P. Webb
23. Pors, N. O. (1990) Employment patterns, the labour market and students' preferences. *Libri*, June, 112–125
24. Webb, S. P. (1987) Approaches to business information in Australia and the United Kingdom: observations and comparisons. *Business Information Review*, July, 29–34

Appendix

Advisory, Conciliation and Arbitration Service
Head Office
27 Wilton Street
London SW1X 7AZ
UK

American Library Association
50 East Huron Street
Chicago IL 60611
USA

ASLIB, The Association for Information Management
20 Old Street
London EC1V 9AP
UK

Aslib Professional Recruitment
20 Old Street
London EC1V 9AP
UK

Australian Information Management Association
c/o Macquarie University Library
Sydney NSW 2109
Australia

British Association for Industrial and Commercial Education
16 Park Crescent
London W1N 4AP
UK

British Institute of Management
Management House
Cottingham Road
Corby
Northants NN17 1TT
UK

Central Office of the Industrial Tribunals
93 Ebury Bridge Road
London SW1W 8RE
UK

Commission for Racial Equality
Elliott House
Allington Street
London SW1E 5EH
UK

Department of Employment
Overseas Labour Section
Block C, Porter Brook House
c/o Moorfoot
Sheffield S1 4PQ
UK

Equal Employment Opportunity Commission
1801 L Street NW
Washington DC 20507
USA

Equal Opportunities Commission
Overseas House
Quay Street
Manchester M3 3HN
UK

Health and Safety Executive
Baynards House
1 Chepstow Place
London W2 4TE
UK

Institute of Directors
116 Pall Mall
London SW1Y 5ED
UK

Institute of Information Scientists
44/45 Museum Street
London WC1A 1LY
UK

Institute of Personnel Management
IPM House
Camp Road
London SW19 4UX
UK

Industrial Society
Peter Runge House
3 Carlton House Terrace
London SW1 5DG
UK

INFOMATCH (Recruitment Agency)
The Library Association
7 Ridgmount Street
London WC1E 7AE
UK

International Federal of Library Associations and Institutions
POB 95312
2509 CH
The Hague
The Netherlands

The Library Association
7 Ridgmount Street
London WC1E 7AE
UK

Local Government Management Board
Arndale House
Arndale Centre
Luton LU1 2TS
UK

New Ways to Work
309 Upper Street
London N1 2TY
UK

Office for Library Personnel Resources
American Library Association
50 East Huron Street
Chicago IL 60611
USA

The Pepperell Department
The Industrial Society
Robert Hyde House
48 Bryanston Square
London W1
UK

Personnel, Training and Education Group
c/o The Library Association
7 Ridgmount Street
London WC1E 7AE
UK

Society for Human Resource Management
606 North Washington Street
Alexandria VA 22314
USA

Special Libraries Association
1700 Eighteenth Street, NW
Washington DC 20009–2508
USA

Task Force Pro Libra Ltd (TFPL)
22 Peter's Lane
London EC1M 6DS
UK

Index